*Cover Image:*

*The original breeding pair,
George and Louisa Parsons, 1870s.
Photo courtesy of Julienne Schofield
and the Parsons family of Victoria.*

*Cover Design:* Rad Young

# Rabbits and other Immigrants:
## *The Alan Parsons story*

A memoir on arriving and thriving in West Australia

Written and researched by Julie Lenora Parsons

Copyright © Julie Parsons, 2023

First published in 2018 by Julie Parsons,
Fremantle, Western Australia.

This edition published: 2023 by Leschenault Press
Leschenault, Western Australia

ISBN: 978-1-923020-42-9 – Paperback
978-1-923020-43-6 – eBook

Editor: Mary Elgar
Book designer: Rad Young
Illustrator: Julie Parsons

The right of Julie Parsons to be identified as author of this work has been asserted by her in accordance with sections 77 and 78 of the copyright, designs and patents act 1988.

All rights reserved. No part of this publication may be reproduced or transmitted in any form or by any means, electronic or mechanical, including photography, recording, or any information storage or retrieval system, without permission in writing from the publisher.

The book is sold subject to the condition that it shall not, by way of trade or otherwise, be lent, resold or otherwise circulated without the publisher's prior consent in any form of binding or cover other than that in which it is published and without a similar condition, including this condition, being imposed on the subsequent purchaser.

# Contents

Preface ............................................................. 7
Acknowledgements ................................................ 9
Forward ........................................................... 10

## *Part One*
### *On arriving in Western Australia: The ancestors*

1. Putting the cart before the horse ........................... 17
2. Leader in farming technology ............................... 45

## *Part Two*
### *On surviving in Western Australia: Alan's life takes shape*

3. The relations and the stutter ............................... 75
4. The getting of wisdom ...................................... 99
5. Alan meets Mavis ........................................... 119
6. All about Mavis ............................................. 149

## *Part Three*
### *On thriving in Western Australia: Parsons in the South West*

7. Everything happens in 10-year cycles ...................... 193
8. Parsons-proof fence ........................................ 221
9. Fun times: all things recreational ......................... 237
10. But wait he's back ......................................... 255

Epilogue .......................................................... 285
Appendices ....................................................... 291
Bibliography ..................................................... 306
Image credits .................................................... 309

# *Preface*

The story starts in England during the 1850s, in a village in Somerset where Thomas Austin engaged farm boys for work on his station 'Barwon Park' in Victoria, Australia. Young George Parsons was one of those boys. Austin also collected English rabbits to take to his station. The rabbits were bred for hunting and released into the wild, quickly spreading across Australia. Young Parsons escaped from the station having endured cruelty there, finding work with a carrier, his future father-in-law, in Portland and surrounds. Parsons bought farming land in Minyip, central Victoria, in 1877. After the Federation Drought in the 1900s, his son made his way beyond the rabbit-proof fence in WA to start a new life in Narrogin.

Alan Parsons was born on the eve of the Great Depression and like his forefathers, was brought up on the land and taught how to supplement income with carting. The family, along with many others, survived the Depression by taking advantage of the commercial benefits of rabbits.

After years of hard work, Alan Parsons gave up farming and, despite a severe speech impediment, set off into the world of selling. He was encouraged by his family's motto, 'hard work always brings good luck'. Alan went on to become one of the most prolific farm machinery and truck dealers in the South West of Western Australia, and on occasion, in Australia; his competition stated they needed a 'Parsons-proof fence' to survive. Alan took his business skills into the community, supporting a number of notable causes where he was able to raise extraordinary funds to the benefit of others.

# *Dedication*

This book is dedicated to those who came from England at the call of Thomas Austin, and the Australian Government, to farm this ancient land. The history within is a gift of remembrance to the descendants of George Parsons (1837-1919) and Louisa Pitts (1848-1935) and in particular to those descendants of their great-grandson, Alan Parsons.

Alan Clifford Parsons
1929 - 2023

# *Acknowledgements*

The book grew out of the many stories told by Alan Parsons, without which the cohesion and links to our past would be lost. We are forever grateful.

Full appreciation goes to all family members and friends of the family, for their support and contributions on various occasions, with particular mentions going to Susan Thompson, Anne Elliott, Anna Haebich, Yvonne Matthews, Peter Clarke, Kester McKay, Diane Davies, Judyth Salom, Graham Drage (Victoria), and special thanks to Julienne Schofield (Victoria) for her extraordinary research into the Parsons and Pitts family history. Both Graham and Julienne are direct descendants from George Parsons in eastern Australia.

Gracious and indebted appreciation also goes to storytellers Mavis and her cousin June, along with support from June's daughter Anne, for her verification through research into the family heritage in chapter's five and six and for her invaluable proof read. Finally, gratitude goes to Mavis and Alan's grandson, Rad Young, for his expertise in book design.

Thanks also go to Mary Elgar of The Memory Scribe elgareditingservices.com for her excellent editing services.

# *Foreword*

Fans of Albert Facey's book A Fortunate Life will find much of interest in this story of the life and times of Alan Parsons. Facey wrote about growing up in the Western Australian Wheatbelt in the decades between the Great War and the end of the 1930s Depression, when he moved to Perth. Alan Parsons is of the next generation. His story follows the ensuing twenty years of families farming in the Wheatbelt until he, too, left in the 1950s with his wife and family to build a new life in the coastal town of Bunbury.

Like the Facey family, the Parsons family moved to Western Australia in the early 1900s to escape ruinous drought and depression in rural Victoria, and to find a better life. They joined thousands of other families establishing farms in the newly opened Wheatbelt. Grandfather George Parsons' knowledge of growing drought-resistant wheat crops in Victoria, shared with other farmers in the Narrogin district, helped them through the lean years that forced many others off the land. Still, it was a hard life, making do with what fate served up and doing backbreaking work for extra cash to survive. Flashes of inspiration and good luck were there too. Family support was essential. Like many farmers during the Depression, Alan's parents faced poverty and hardship. However, coupled with this was the necessity to leave Alan with his aunts, uncles and grandparents to enable his schooling. Alan built on the resulting enriching experiences throughout his life.

In the late 1940s, after a whirlwind romance that began across the counter of the Ford Dealership in Corrigin, Alan married Mavis Horner (in 1951). Together they entered into the 'A&M' business partnership which was to become iconic throughout the South West. Mavis's creative, British-born family had experienced tragedy and loss on the land but Mavis applied herself with great style to the role of farmer's wife and mother. Then came the shift to the mechanisation of farming on large tracts of land, which precipitated the couple's decision to sell their Corrigin farm of ten years and move to Bunbury. Thus began a whole new phase of their lives that is retold in the book, as they established themselves as a prominent business and artistic family in the Bunbury district.

Ironically, it was Alan's new business venture selling International Harvester farm machinery that gave him his first break. The combination of good luck, being in the right place at the right time, family traits of hard work and sharing knowledge and ideas with others got him past the post.

It was about this time that I first met Alan Parsons in the family's home in Mangles Street, Bunbury. Alan was in the games room behind the bar serving drinks to friends who were playing pool and sharing 'Dad' jokes. We immediately dubbed him 'Big Al'. He didn't seem to mind and the name has stuck over the years. As Julie's friend, I was made to feel welcome and at home, a part of the family. Mavis had raised her daughters with her gifts of creativity and humour and behind her with fortitude was Big Al, big in stature, big in hospitality and big in visions.

Like everything associated with Big Al, there are no half measures, as is apparent in this book. Big Al's creative spirit is his daughter Julie who did the research, collected the images, interviewed family and friends and wrote the book with passion and humour, with contributions from the rest of the family. The result is a tapestry of stories about the life and times of Alan Parsons and the places and people swirling around him as his life shifts and changes; his family in Narrogin and Corrigin, and his friends in Bunbury and throughout the South West.

The Big Al games room at Mangles Street is no more. It initially disappeared under the weight of Mavis and Julie's theatre costumes, its pool table unashamedly used as a cutting table, and then was finally discarded with a house move. But not before Alan's active community fundraising secured substantial funds for the creation of the Bunbury Regional Entertainment Centre. Alan's capacity to raise funds for the community is considerable and significant, with projects ranging from the introduction of the life saving 'Jaws of Life', to research in South West health being notable amongst them.

In later years, this modest couple applied themselves to realising their dream home, enjoying picturesque views of the outer harbour and marina in Koombana Bay with easy walking and cycling access to the city centre.

Anna Haebich
John Curtin Distinguished Professor
Curtin University

# Part One

## On arriving In Western Australia: The ancestors

*Horse and cart, with teams of horses used by Narrogin farmers in the early 1900s*

Alan Clifford Parsons aged 3, 1932.
Born 12th of February 1929,
Narrogin, Western Australia

## CHAPTER ONE

# *In 1929 the New York stock market collapsed; that same year Alan Parsons was born*

### *Putting the cart before the horse*

With the 1930s Great Depression changing lives, Alan was living with his parents on his grandfather's farm in the central Wheatbelt of Western Australia. This is Alan's first significant memory:

> *I must have been four years of age. Dad had taken his team of eight horses about a mile to the paddock where he was ploughing, which he was doing every day for a few weeks. He normally walked the horses home at lunch time, fed and watered them, had his own lunch, then did the same in the afternoon. This day he didn't come home at lunchtime.*
> 
> *At about 3pm, Mum realised something was wrong, so she and I walked out to where he'd been ploughing, only to find him lying next to the plough, the team of horses still coupled to it, ready to go. Apparently, when he told the horses 'to go' early that morning, all their pulling power took over but the main swing, made from bush timber, broke and then came back and hit Dad's leg, breaking the bone.*

*He had to lay there all that time, in pain, talking to the horses so they would not take off. By the time we found him, it was lightly raining and Mum had to leave me there while she quickly walked for help, roughly three miles. Help arrived about two hours later, in the form of my grandfather, my uncle and an old Chevy truck. Dad was loaded onto the back of the truck, in agony, and off he went to hospital over sixteen miles of corrugated roads. Uncle Bert then took the horses home with us walking through the rain*

*George F. Parsons' Chevy Truck, c.1930*

Alan's childhood memory began in the Western Australian Wheatbelt, on a property outside Corrigin, in the early 1930s. The situation in rural Western Australia was dire, despite WA farmers producing a bumper crop in 1931. Sadly, because of the Great Depression, wheat prices simply collapsed. The more militant wheat growers formed a union and attempted a strike in 1932. According to documents in the State Library of WA, 'they did this by withholding the delivery of crops and preventing the forced sale of bankrupt properties through disrupting auctions'.

*Team of eight plough horses, each with their own unique character, Corrigin c1920*

With farming life beset with difficulties and a scarcity of jobs, change was afoot. In 1933, when Alan was aged four, his parents, Alma and Clifford Parsons, went to work on the farm that Alan's grandfather, George F. Parsons, managed with his other sons, Fred, Stan, and Bert or Treb (Bert spelt backwards). The farm was situated at Bendering, east of Corrigin. The sons came, then went, both supporting their parents and being supported by them in times of need, as was the case with Cliff. The Parsons' ancestors' journey to reach this point had been long, desperate and arduous.

In the mid-1800s, Alan's great-grandfather, George Parsons Snr, a 16-year-old migrant from England, found himself adrift in Australia after escaping from succumbed (indentured) employment on a station near Geelong. Having made good his escape, and after some twenty or so years, he occupied his own acreage on newly opened-up land in and around the wetlands of Warracknabeal, situated in middle Victoria and often referred to as part of the Western District.

But why and how was he in Australia in the first place? This question has been asked from time to time by various descendants over the generations.

Leading up to the 1980s, two of his grandchildren tried to piece together what they had heard and thought to be true of their great-grandparent's story. Les Sharp, one of these great-grandchildren, researched what he believed to be truths, but which ended up exposing more questions than answers. Nothing seemed to add up until Julienne Schofield, also a direct descendant, took up the gauntlet. Her advantage was her competency as a family historian.

Curiously, and concurrently, in the 1980s, independent Parsons' family reunions were organised by Alan Parsons in Western Australia and the family in Victoria. Alan organised a river cruise to Sandalford Winery. He invited all 104 Western Australian descendants of George Parsons Snr. 92 attended. On the other side of the country, the Parsons descendants of Victoria hired a football oval and had over 3,000 attend the reunion.

Julienne Schofield began to work on the perplexing puzzle of George Parsons' journey from England to Australia; it was no easy matter but some thirty years later her findings have finally contributed to the following story.

## *Understanding the family roots*

The story starts in the village of Baltonsborough (a borough designates a self-governing, walled town), which lies some six kilometres south-east of Glastonbury, in Somerset. Its south-western boundary is the River Brue and the village has views towards the Tor and the Mendip Hills.

At its centre, the village has a post office shop, public house and a village hall. Surrounding the village are farms. Baltonsborough also has a magnificent church, which contains the graves of many Parsons ancestors. The Church of St Dunstan is a homage to Saint Dunstan, who was born in Baltonsborough and is the patron saint of blacksmiths, silversmiths and goldsmiths. The significance of this is remarkable; just ten kilometres away a desperate mother left a newborn on the doorstep of the local blacksmith shop in Pylle. It was January 1771, and this baby, just a few hours old, was George's grandmother. She was named Mary 'Smith', no doubt referring to where she was found at the smithy.

In 1799, Mary Smith married Joseph Porter, an agricultural labourer in Ditcheat, eleven kilometres from Baltonsborough. Together they had eight children; their fifth child, Harriet Porter, married James Parsons and they moved to Baltonsborough where he lived. Harriet and James produced ten children, one of which would go to Australia. His name was George Parsons.

The implication of Saint Dunstan (c.909-988) being born in Baltonsborough and the resurgence of Christianity, may have some relevance to the surname of Parsons finding its way to the Glastonbury area. 'Parsons' is an occupationally derived name originally meaning someone who served the parish priest/parson or the child of a parson. Dunstan became the Abbot of Glastonbury where he began to re-examine Christianity. He ardently pursued his revived reverent approach, ultimately becoming the Archbishop of Canterbury in 960. Having notably reformed the English Church, Dunstan was canonised in 1029. His sainthood kept him popular for a number of centuries. Other than his early presence in Glastonbury, and the possibility of this eventually attracting the emergence of the Parsons surname in the area, this connection of faith in the patron saint of blacksmiths, by Mary Smith's anonymous mother is blessed and so the Parsons lineage continues.

The archaeological finds, within a 10-kilometre radius of Baltonsborough, reveal a magnitude of items and sites rich in history ranging from Mesolithic, Neolithic, Bronze Age, Iron Age, Roman, Celtic, Viking, Medieval and post-Medieval (the soil in Somerset holds a mesmerising soup of mixed cultures and ancestry). The Church of St Dunstan was built in the 15th century, and George, and his family before him, were almost certainly christened and/or buried there.

George Parsons' paternal grandparents were James Parsons (Snr) and Mary Young. George's father, also named James, was one of five children. There is no marriage record of George's father, James Parsons (Jnr), but there is evidence that he devoted his life to Harriet Porter, beginning around 1830 with the birth of their first child. George Parsons was their fifth child, more than likely born in 1838.

***ill i:*** *Thomas Austin, originally from the village of Baltonsborough, owner of Barwon Park, Victoria. Graphite drawing after the portrait In Victoria and its Metropolis, Past and Present.*

The UK 1851 Census shows George was still in Britain although no longer living with his parents. It states his age as eleven and that George and his sixteen-year-old sister Mary, were working and living at Cockmill Lane, Pilton, on a large farm, ten kilometres from Baltonsborough. The farm is now the centre of the Glastonbury Festival, in an area where the Love Fields of the 21st century takes place.

In this census George was described as a farm servant and Mary as a house servant. George probably started work aged ten, because that is the age the family has always referenced for when he left home. The 104-acre farm was run by an unmarried man, Mr Christ. Moody, then aged 62.

Just three years later, on the eve of George's sixteenth birthday in September 1854, he boarded the ship Orwell with a small group of 'Farm Boys' from Baltonsborough. They were selected for Mr Thomas Austin, who was originally from Baltonsborough, but living in rural Victoria, Australia. The boys arrived in Williamstown, Melbourne, at the end of 1854. George may have befriended a boy called Alfred (Giddins perhaps). Although the family often referred to this young man as his brother, there is no evidence that any of George's brothers left the UK. The two boys were assigned to work on Thomas Austin's farming property, some 29,000 acres at the time.

This vast property, which evolved into the 12,000-hectare station called Barwon Park, was situated 40 km from Geelong, approximately where the town of Winchelsea now stands. Thomas Austin and his brother James, who also hailed from Baltonsborough, arrived in Tasmania in 1831 where they began farming. The first Austin to find his way to Van Diemen's Land was their Uncle, James Austin, who had arrived as a convict. The brothers crossed Bass Strait to the mainland in 1837. As squatters, they took up land in the western district of Victoria and are now considered significant pioneer pastoralists, Thomas Austin being more significant for all the wrong reasons

# *Did a young George Parsons arrive in Australia with the rabbits?*

The notoriety of Thomas Austin cannot go unmentioned. Austin had a passion for hunting and although his property was a successful sheep grazing and horse training farm, he added hunting to the agenda, attracting English aristocrats like the Duke of Edinburgh. It is said the Duke shirked his formal engagements in favour of the hunt, and in 1867 experienced his most successful hunt at Barwon Park, shooting 450 rabbits.

*ill ii: Graphite drawing after engraving by N Chevalier, of
The Duke of Edinburgh rabbit shooting at Barwon Park, Victoria, 1867.*

Austin's vision was praised by the Acclimatisation Society of Victoria, which he joined to further his hobby and fulfil his intention to stock the countryside with his favourite English hunt critters. He industriously introduced many species from England including hares, blackbirds, and thrushes. He also initiated a breeding program of English rabbits and partridges.

Thomas Austin asked his nephew, William Austin, who was still living in Baltonsborough, to put together a shipment to Australia for his beloved acclimatisation program and passion for hunting. The request included twelve grey rabbits, five hares, seventy-two partridges and some sparrows. But William was unable to source twelve grey rabbits so he added some domestic rabbits to complete the request. Reputedly, the wild rabbit from Scotland, with its upright ears and excellent burrowing techniques was also added to the mix.

The rabbit interbreeding program at Barwon Park, produced a very sturdy rabbit. Apparently, in October 1859, Austin released 24 breeding rabbits into the wild for hunting. Surprisingly, other farmers, who up until then may have only kept a few caged rabbits as a food source, were also given breeding pairs by Austin and began to release them onto their properties.

This was more successful than any previous attempt to introduce rabbits, and occurred 40 years prior to the first rabbit-proof fence being erected in Western Australia (1902-07); at 1,832 kilometre in length, the rabbit-proof fence is the longest fence in the world.

By the time of the Great Depression in the 1930s, rabbits had passed through three lines of rabbit-proof fences and were proving to be a valuable food source for George Parsons' descendants in Western Australia.

Although ultimately (and ironically) it was a beneficial outcome for George's descendants, working for Thomas Austin in the 1850s was not a pleasant experience for young George. It seems Alfred and George may have been on the receiving end of some very harsh treatment, whereupon they determined to run away from Barwon Park. Exactly when and where they went, and what they did, will remain a mystery but it is known they parted company and never saw each other again.

## *Was George Parsons who he said he was?*

Julienne Schofield asks this question from the outset because nothing added up until several years later, when she could find some evidence of his movements and activities.

A question of age: Julienne found that George apparently went to Otago in New Zealand on the Oscar in December 1861. The shipping records stated his age as eighteen (implying he was born in 1843), but christening documents state he was baptised in 1839. He returned in January 1862 on the Aldinga.

In his possession was a gold nugget, which he kept and had made into a beautiful brooch. He presented this to his bride, Louisa Pitts, whom he met at Wattle Hill, five kilometres from the centre of Portland, Victoria. Three years after his return from New Zealand, in 1865, the couple were married in Portland. On the wedding certificate, he claimed to be aged 25 (his wife Louisa was 18), making his birth year 1840. However, this was just the beginning.

Julienne Schofield followed up every possibility. George's death certificate stated he spent 64 years in the Colony, which indicates he came out from England in 1844. She discovered the following information, held at Portland History House, that confirmed George returned from New Zealand c.1862 and was living in Portland, where he apparently got into a little trouble: on the Burgess Electoral Roll of 1862, George rented a horse paddock and in 1868 he appeared in Court for mistreating a horse; he was fined 5s and 2s 6d costs. Police Constable Cobb was the prosecutor.

With that sorted, and after his marriage to Louisa Pitts in 1865, Julienne notes the following:

*After their marriage in Portland they drove a dray and three horses on their honeymoon to Mt Gambier. After George had worked around Mt Gambier for a while he began carting stone for the construction of some of Mt Gambier's principal buildings. In 1874 George and his wife selected land at Minyip, then known only as 'Burnt Hut'. In those days, they had very friendly Aborigines nearby.*

## *And just who was Louisa Pitts?*

Louisa Pitts was born on 11 April 1848, in Keinton, Somerset, England, to Frederick Richard and Julia Pitts (née Gaylor). Her birthplace is eerily close to George's. The Pitts family travelled to Australia on the Nestor, in 1854. Louisa, then aged six, was to be the third of seven siblings.

To understand why people were leaving the United Kingdom during the 1850s is best explored by understanding the prevailing conditions in Somerset. These could have applied to young George Parsons and his friend Alfred, when they left Baltonsborough, near Keinton, for similar reasons. The year the boys left was also 1854, but they boarded another ship called the Orwell.

The changing work environment around Somerset had threatened the livelihood of families for some time. The traditional cottage industry of the region was spinning and knitting stockings for a Glastonbury manufacturer, but home industries such as these were hit hardest by the introduction of large factories in the Midlands, and a massive industrialisation shift was taking place. This had a knock-on effect.

The surname 'Pitt' or 'Pitts' possibly relates to the once-thriving, limestone quarries around Keinton. The quality limestone was used for building and provided work for the village inhabitants both in mining and carting it. It is understood that very few worked as farm labourers. With the limestone pits emptying, change loomed.

In addition to the employment changes during the 1850s, there were also massive changes in the weather; crops were threatened with temperatures reaching 90 degrees (fahrenheit), alternating with severe frosts and freezing conditions. Even the journey by these West Country families to the Nestor, which lay anchored in Plymouth, was made in extreme conditions. The Nestor set sail with 193 emigrants.

Travelling on a sailing ship in those days was often fraught with danger, frequently with half-a-dozen or so deaths on board. These gruelling sea journeys, towards the promise of a new life in Australia, offered a better, hope-filled opportunity when compared with remaining in England. There were three infant deaths reported on the Nestor, so given Louisa's young age, she was indeed a lucky one.

Julienne Schofield found that the Pitts family emigrated under the Victorian

Government of Australia's assisted passage scheme, and according to Florence Chuk in her 1987 book The Somerset Years, the following is what assisted passage meant:

> [The Pitts] emigrated under the assisted passage scheme where they paid a small deposit, but the government paid the passage fees, provided provisions, medical attendance, cooking utensils at the depot and on board the ship. Additionally, new mattresses, bolsters, blankets and counterpanes, canvas bags to contain linen, knives and forks, spoons, metal plates and drinking mugs, which articles will be given after arrival in the colony to the emigrants who have behaved well on their voyage.

The barque Nestor had been in service for 14 years. When she arrived at Portland, Australia, two ships were already moored with a third arriving the following day carrying another 250 immigrants. The rush for gold was in full swing and because of this the Nestor immediately lost some of its crew to gold fever. But intrigue followed with an event which saw her unable to leave the Australian shoreline at all. The following is part of the story according to the Australian National Shipwreck Database:

> After arriving at Portland, the NESTOR discharged its passengers and was destined to sail for Madras with a cargo of Railway Iron for the Madras railway, when on Friday, 27 October 1854, the master of the vessel had a cannon fired indicating that the vessel was in distress. Observers on shore noticed that the ship's anchors had been slipped and it was drifting ashore. The Harbour Master boarded the vessel and was informed that the Captain had ordered the vessel to be sounded and discovered 6' of water in the hold. The Captain then ordered the vessel to be driven ashore in order to preserve life. The NESTOR grounded just off the jetty. A Marine Enquiry held on the 28 October 1854, found that the loss of the vessel was due to three auger holes being bored through the hull near the sternpost. Captain Brown, and two others, Robertson and Jully were charged with feloniously scuttling the barque NESTOR. The charges were later dropped due to lack of evidence.

Two Pitts families travelled together on the Nestor and settled in Wattle Hill, five kilometres out of Portland. This may have been because another Pitts family had arrived on the Severn in 1846, and were already settled in Wattle Hill, Portland.

By 1862, Louisa's father, Frederick Pitts, owned a team of bullocks and was carting wool from the sheep stations to the wool-stores. He was often away for six months at a time. It is probable young George Parsons was also doing this work, possibly even working for Pitts on occasion, which may offer some explanation of how he met Pitts' daughter, Louisa.

After George and Louisa Parsons married, they, along with three other young honeymooners, set off for Mt Gambier to work on the road, the Parsons with a dray and three horses. Curiously, George, not unlike the Pitts family from Somerset, set about carting stone, which was used for some of Mt Gambier's principal buildings. George went on to own six acres in Casterton, 202 kilometres from Mt Gambier. Owning this property gave him a resting place between, and during, carting trips.

Ten years later, George, Louisa and their three children loaded their possessions into a wagon and began the journey to take up land at Burnt Hut, in the Warracknabeal area. Minyip (Burnt Hut), was to become their family's home in the years to come. Warracknabeal is some 266kms inland from Wattle Hill, Portland, and far from Louisa's family of origin. The journey in part is described in an article in the Warracknabeal Herald, dated the 8th of July 1932;

*A REMARKABLE LIFE: REMINISCES OF THE EARLY DAYS. In April 1875 Mrs. Parsons and her husband, and three children packed up at Mt Gambier, and set out with their few belongings, implements etc. on a wagon, and four horses to take up land in the Wimmera, camping en route, their first camp in the Wimmera was the site just outside Horsham (now the bridge over the Wimmera River) there were very few shops in Horsham in those days, but a few articles were obtained at Langlands, and Browns. At Dooen, heavy rain began to fall, and the horses being all heavily shod, the sticky earth soon began to clog their feet, and several times in the mud Mr. Parsons had to leave the wagon, and clean the horses' feet to allow them to proceed. (Early residents will remember the tenacity of the black soil in those days.)*

The couple's eldest son James, scarcely aged seven, rode his pony some distance behind; his charge was to herd just four head of cattle. Presumably he was tracking the wagon wheels across the landscape as there were no roads of consequence at that time. James had his own food supply and slept with his pony under the trees at night. When the rest of the family arrived at their destination young James was nowhere to be seen. To all intents and purposes, he was missing. His father made camp and left his wife and two young children in the tent and then set off into the night to find the intrepid James and the cattle.

According to Louisa, a number of Aborigines gathered around the tent trying to comprehend why they were there. However, it was only curiosity that had lured them as no harm came to the trio inside. Meanwhile utterly exhausted and unable to proceed, the boy and the cattle had stopped to rest some considerable miles back. George eventually found his son and the cattle but was compelled to see the night out where he found them.

Working a selection of land was often times much harder than expected and many, out of sheer desperation, abandoned their selection. Water shortage was frequently a problem on the Parsons' selection, with George travelling ten kilometres each day to Yarriambiack Creek at Kewell, to allow the cattle to drink. Once the crops began to produce, George carted the wheat to Stawell some 76 kilometres away. He would leave home on Monday and return on Saturday with a wagon load of supplies.

The astonishing perseverance of Louisa is well documented by her granddaughter, Myrtle Gerdsen. In 1875, during a particularly wet winter, Myrtle tells us the family was still living in the tent and Louisa was expecting her fourth child. At this stage, George took the floor out of the wagon and set it into the tent to provide a dry area for the birth. In an unusual gesture, some Aborigines had gathered nearby, perhaps understanding the impending situation. But things could not have gone to plan, because their fourth child was registered as being born in early August in Horsham, over 50 kilometres away, and the wet winter would have surely required the wagon's floor to be reinstated to its rightful position for the trip. However, seven of their fourteen children were successfully born at Minyip.

Without a doctor in the area, Mrs Smith, a local nurse, had agreed to attend one of Louisa's birthings when the time came; and come it did in 1882 with Louisa sending

George off in a hurry to find the said woman. Meanwhile, Louisa pressed on with her bread baking until forced to pause while birthing the child. She immediately sent her eldest sons off on an errand, but soon realised there was more than one child on the way. The boys, who interpreted the event as their mother dying on the kitchen floor, ran to find their father. The boys later noted twins were rampant that year with nearly every ewe birthing twin lambs.

*ill iii: The old wagon on the Minyip property with the faint memory of Martha doing a jig to entertain her siblings. A family photograph of the old wagon on the original property inspired the graphite drawing.*

Sadly, with no permanent medical help in the area, when an accident took place time would take its toll. Whilst travelling from Casterton to Bungalally, near Horsham by wagon one day, Martha, their third child, was doing a jig on the back to entertain her siblings when the wheel hit a stump and she fell off. The fall broke her pelvis but with no doctor she went untreated until the family was finally able to see one. But it was too late and she lived the rest of her life managing the crippling consequences. She was very immobile with a twisted leg. Eventually a built-up boot was added but she seldom went outdoors. Martha remained single.

Julienne describes the dam as being dug with pick, shovel and wheel barrow. She also informs us of the construction technique used on the building on the left in the photograph which is the house George built in 1875 (the house on the right was built later):

*The building was constructed by posting the ground, then branches cut from trees on the property, fixed to the posts then filled in between with clay making it weather proof. Camp ovens were dug into the ground behind the far side wall, in these they baked their bread etc., these ovens still remain in their original position in 1983 when the property was visited by the late Les Sharp. The building also remains on the property, now used as a barn and workshop.*

It was a tough start with their first crop only returning seed; in 1888, a horrific storm completely flattened their best crop. But it was the trivial things that were sent to test them — with the summer came hordes of dreaded blowflies, which in turn brought eye infections called Sandy Blight and other eye problems for everyone at some point.

This wonderful woman not only bore fourteen children, but frequently walked the seven miles to Burnt Hut (later called Minyip) and back, often times carrying a baby or two on her back. She would not only have carried or managed small children, but also the eggs her poultry had surrendered, and the butter she made after milking the cow each day. Added to this, every fortnight Louisa turned 250 lbs (113 kgs) of flour into bread in small camp ovens. She sold what she could to purchase other supplies for her rapidly growing family, which she then carried back to her home. Once home, Louisa set about preparing the continuous flow of meals including morning and afternoon teas. At lunchtime, the midday meal was also carried out to the workers in the paddocks. Louisa did the same walk with the morning and afternoon teas. Louisa would tie the cups to her forearms in order to tote the hot tea and various other refreshments.

No doubt due to Louisa's good mothering and George's good husbandry, only one child died in infancy; the other thirteen children lived long lives, and like the rabbits reproduced far and wide.

Soon a long dining table, easily able to seat twenty, replaced the wagon floor.

*George and Louisa Parsons and the dam they dug by hand c.1870*

Music too entered the enlarged house, as each and every family member learned to play an assortment of instruments of their choice. A music room was purpose built for the sing-a-long gatherings.

## *Hard work was the essence of the prosperity that eventually came their way*

It is said George returned to England to visit his mother and sisters, possibly sometime after the birth of their thirteenth child in 1890, and before the birth of their last child in 1895, the year his mother passed away aged 85. Apparently, his mother did not recognise him, whereupon he revealed a boyhood scar on his leg as confirmation. This she recognised and immediately accepted him as her son. Upon returning to Australia, it seems his mother sent an annual box full of Christmas cards, personally addressed to every member of the ever-expanding family.

Julienne Schofield's summary of George's life on the land after his marriage to Louisa Pitts in 1865 was this:

> *For ten years after his marriage George ran a carrier business in the Portland, Casterton and Mt Gambier regions. George made his selection of land at Minyip at 10.45 am on 12 October 1874, before J. Langlands JP, at Horsham. His requirements to make selection were for him to: Dig a trench not less than 2' long and 6" wide and 4" deep in each corner and in the direction of the continuing sides, and place a conspicuous post or cairns of stones with notices thereon. (The land act was formed in 1869 and the selector could select a block of not more than 320 acres, George's selections were 319 acres, three roods, 10 perches in the Parish of Kewell East, Allotment 111.) The lease was recommended on 18 December 1874, signed by E. Smith, and was sent to Casterton for signature on the 9th of January 1875. The payment for the block was £320, payable every half year, being the first day of February and the first day of August each year.*

*The fee of £8 16s 0d mileage was paid on 26 October 1874.*
*1. That the Selector live on the land for 2½ to 3 years.*
*2. Pay 2s per acre per year.*
*3. Land had to be fenced, also had to make improvements to the value of £1 per acre to his selection in the term of three years. If at the end of three years the selector had met all these requirements he was allowed to apply for a lease or if he could pay the full price of a £1 per acre he could apply for freehold title.*
*George Parsons met all these requirements and was able to pay the £320, therefore held freehold title in his first three years. The improvements that he made during his first three years were:*
*Erected 334 chain of post and wire fencing at a cost of 10s per chain.*
*Total cost £164.*
*Cultivated and sowed 20 acres of wheat, yielding 12 bushels per acre at a cost of £1 per acre.*
*The second year he sowed 40 acres, yielding another 12 bushels.*
*In the third year he sowed 50 acres, yielding another 12 bushels.*
*Built a dwelling house, 4 rooms of hardwood and iron, in an area measuring 30 feet x 15 feet and at a cost of £40.*
*Excavated a dam 848 cubic yards, length 58 feet x 48 feet x 8 feet deep at a cost of £42.*
*George dug this dam with the use of a pick, shovel and barrow. The dam is still on the property.*
*Built a logged tank, 13 feet x 13 feet x 15 feet, at a cost of £12.*
*Built a barn, chaff house and shed at a cost of £12. The barn is still on the property.*
*Also spent £27 on a garden.*
*In total £409 was spent.*

George purchased property at Sheep Hills c.1890, where he built a big home and many sheds. He farmed there, so it is said, until each son was set up on his own farming property, enabling George and Louisa to retire into a home in Warracknabeal (situated on the banks of the Yarriambiack Creek, 330 km north-west of Melbourne). George died in 1919 as an honoured pioneer of the Shire of Yarriambiack (originally the County of Borung until 1938, then the Shire of Warracknabeal until 1995).

*George and Louisa Parsons with daughter Martha, and son Frank at their retirement home in Anderson St Warracknabeal 1909. In 2017 the house was still lived in by a descendant of George and Louisa Parsons, great grandson, Bruce Parsons.*

*Map of western Victoria*

The Warracknabeal area was opened up about 40 years beforehand. According to the Yarriambiack Heritage Study, clearing the fragile wetlands immediately around the Yarriambiack Creek meant the area became prone to sudden localised flooding, particularly during a La Niña event, with Warracknabeal flooding in 1909. It is understood that the Shire of Yarriambiack was once under a vast shallow sea.

Initially the land was uncleared native vegetation used as pastoral runs, until the rabbit made good his territory after 1860. Farmers aided and abetted this by clearing the land for grazing sheep in the 1850s, and then for growing wheat on large acreages in the 1880s, which was when the land became subdivided into rectangular allotments. This consequently allowed a grid pattern to be reinforced by tracks and roads, particularly over the Yarriambiack Creek area, creating a vulnerable situation. As the groundwater of the ancient sea got closer to the surface, due to wind, rain and flooding washing away the topsoil, the salt rose and the land became prone to soil salinity. Once this was understood it was addressed, but not before some of the earlier farmers experienced loss of land and income.

A young thirteen-year-old boy arrived in the Warracknabeal district in 1893. Keith Hofmaier later interviewed him for his book, Mallee Memories. The boy became Mr P.O. Hopkins, a retired Warracknabeal Nurseryman. Hopkins recalled the beauty and diversity of the area in the 1890s before farming made its mark:

*I was always keen on nature, and the Mallee at that time was a paradise for a nature lover. I saw any number of kangaroos, emus and dingoes. The birdlife was wonderful. Mallee hens, bronzewing pigeons and duck were plentiful. The cockatoos, parrots and parakeets – many kinds – were a sight to behold! Most of them disappeared when the land was cleared, as did many of the native plants and wildflowers of the Mallee. Ask any of the old farmers – you never see any of the wildflowers they saw in profusion when they were children. Have you ever seen a glade so thick with paper sunrays – so white with everlasting daisies it looked like snow? Have you ever seen sweeps of wild sweet peas – so close they looked pools of water – and their perfume ... it's unforgettable! Strawflowers, bachelor's buttons, fringe lilies and little orchids – where do you ever see them now – the greenhoods, spider and wild duck shaped blooms – all gone.*

George and Louisa celebrating their daughter Maude's wedding at Sheep Hills homestead 1907. George is standing behind and between Louisa who is seated next to her bridesmaid daughters Lillian and Annie, while it is said the Parsons boys are in the back row. Third from the right in the front row is Ede Parsons (née Bland) nursing Cliff Parsons aged two. George F. Parsons (Jnr) appears to be standing next to Ede's father Joseph Bland. Ede's mother Emily Bland, is the fifth from the right in the second row.

George Parsons' gravesite is a shrine to a man who made a name for himself as a principled and valued pioneer in the establishment of the Warracknabeal district (now in the Yarriambiack Shire).

## *Mystery man*

PARSONS: George, b.1838-1919, England, son of James PARSONS & Harriet PORTER, d. Warracknabeal, Victoria, m. 1865 to Louisa PITTS c.1848-1935, b. Somersetshire, England, to Frederick Richard PITTS & Julia GAYLOR, d. Warracknabeal, Vic., children at Portland, Sandford, Casterton, Minyip and WA.

The family story has always suggested George was looked after by a family who ran a carrier business using horses, drays and wagons. Perhaps when George ran away from Barwon Park he found his way to Wattle Hill, home of the pioneer Pitts family, a mere 112 kms away?

This fragile entry into Australian life, suggests the loss of his family presented a challenge to his identity. George, with strong family ethics, ardently set about forging his place in Australia, and he soon anchored himself in the Warracknabeal area. George was one of the first revered pioneer settlers.

*Monument to George and Louisa Parsons in Warracknabeal. Photo: Julienne Schofield*

## *Eight years after celebrating Maude's wedding*

A lavish article appeared in the Warracknabeal Herald on the 3rd of December 1915, stating that pioneers, George and Louisa Parsons, were celebrating their 50th wedding anniversary. The article said George arrived in Victoria in 1854 from Somersetshire in England and that having found himself in the newly opened-up farming land in the district, at 23 he met and married the 18-year-old Louisa, coincidently also heralding from Somersetshire. The article bore witness to the couple's well-earned respect as significant pioneers in north-west rural Victoria (see Appendix I).

They also attempted to populate the district, producing some fourteen children with twelve listed in the 1915 article as still living. The article inferred all but one remained in the community. They supported their parents and each other well, through both difficult and successful agricultural times over the next fifty years.

*Louisa Parsons on her 75th birthday seated centre surrounded by 13 of her surviving children, 1922*
*Seated: Annie (Sharpe née Parsons), George F., Louisa, James, Martha (single)*
*Middle row: Walter, Maude (Jenkins née Parsons), Edward (twin),*
*Lillian (Newell née Parsons), Alfred (twin), Herbert*
*Back Row: Charles, Frank and Arthur*

## *George Frederick Parsons (Jnr) and Emily Edith 'Ede' Parsons (née Bland)*

PARSONS: George Frederick, b.1871-1941, Sandford, Victoria, son of George PARSONS & Louisa PITTS, d. Corrigin, WA., m. 1894 to Emily Edith BLAND 1872-1958, b. Geelong, Vic, to Joseph BLAND and Emily MANN, d. Perth, WA.

When George F. and Emily (known as Ede) married, they apparently farmed at Beulah, north of Warracknabeal for a couple of years. They then came to Warracknabeal with their children in 1898, and according to descendant Graham Drage, stayed until 1905. It appears the family pioneered a property at Lake Whitton (not far from Warracknabeal). Overall, George F. Parsons farmed about the district for approximately fourteen years. He and Edith are officially cited and remembered amongst the Sandford Settlers and Pioneers, Wannon River, south-west Victoria, Australia.

Initially, vast runs of land in this area were taken up by squatters for their sheep. In one case, the Henty family, had, over time, dispersed the vast sheep runs amongst each of the Henty brothers. John Henty occupied Sandford and Runnymede. However, the prolonged drought and rabbit plagues of 1895–1904, often called the Federation Drought, tested the survival of sheep on these extensive land runs. Farmers like George F. and Ede Parsons, who were 'share farming', used the Henty land to grow their crops. Don Garden writes about the dramatic climatic event *The Federation Drought of 1895-1903, El Niño and Society in Australia* (2010):

The length and severity of the Federation Drought make it one of the most significant natural events in Australia's European history and, given the number of human deaths and amount of damage to human property and endeavour especially from the accompanying heatwaves and bushfires, it can be collectively classed as one of Australia's gravest natural disasters.

In 1908, the Henty family subdivided the last remaining big runs; the lots were small and attracted dairy farmers and the like. This, and past events, may have created the opportunity for George F. and Edith to move on to buying their own land.

*ill iv:* In the 1890s the ever-increasing rabbit population had advanced to plague proportions. Between the rabbits and the Federation Drought (1895-1903) farmers faced their greatest challenges. The drought broke with the highest rainfalls on record, followed by flash flooding.

*George and Edith Parsons on their wedding day in 1894*

## CHAPTER TWO

# *"I always thought the Parsons' were battlers not industry leaders"*
### *Graham Drage*

## *A leader in farming technology*

Evidence shows that in the early 1890s Frederick George Parsons (known as George F. Parsons Jnr) and his wife Edith Emily (nee Bland) owned and farmed 652 acres west of Beulah. It is probable they were the original selectors. Their first two children were born there. But the most surprising discovery has been George's innovative approach to his farming practice.

Keith Hofmaier's, Mallee Memories, recounts an interview with Mr P.O. Hopkins, the retired Warracknabeal Nurseryman who arrived in Beulah West in 1893 at age 13:

*I remember Mr. Parsons getting a "sowing machine" to sow the wheat. It was the first out there at the time and farmers from miles around came to inspect it. Before this, the first Mallee farmers sprinkled the wheat by hand, or broadcast it from a container slung around the neck or over the shoulders. This new machine was a mechanical broadcaster, which was driven from a wheel of a cart or a dray. Of course the grain had to be harrowed in or covered afterwards;*

*but the wide sweep spread by the broadcaster was an enormous improvement on hand spreading the seed. The combined seed and fertilizer drill followed soon after for accurate sowing in rows; but it was a very costly machineat the time.*

The couple sold the property to their neighbours sometime before 1900 and appeared to move to the Warracknabeal area where George Snr was farming on his Sheep Hills property. Four more children were born in the Warracknabeal region. It is possible George F. Jnr entered share farming (or farmed under a lease agreement).

It is also entirely possible that George F. Jnr's considerable investment in the "sowing machine' may have financially undermined their farming practice in Beulah. This and a string of unexpected environmental and other events may have caused the family to consider leaving Victoria some eight years later.

## *Becoming Western Australian*

George Frederick Jnr (one of George F. Snr's thirteen children) and Emily Edith 'Ede' (née Bland) left Warracknabeal c.1908 with their six children: Ivy, Les, Fred, Ella, Stan and Cliff. (Cliff, b.1905, and the youngest of the four sons, was Alan's father.) The story is vague but somehow, they obtained some land in Narrogin, WA, which they called 'Highfield'.

The Western Australian Government offered land grants to potential farmers whereby they paid settlers to clear the land thus opening it up for wheat farming. The government paid approximately twenty shillings for every acre cleared and were strict about the time limits required to do so. They also contributed to fencing and general improvements, including loans for stock and machinery. The scheme meant the money paid to the settlers was considered a loan. At the end of the year, a mortgage of the full amount was taken out against the property. The benefit was that the money was lent interest-free and the settlers could pay it back over twenty-five years. But even better, no repayments were to be made for the first five years. It was done this way to give the settlers sufficient time to set the property up for producing. It was indeed a very appealing scheme because land could be taken up with little or no money. People came from everywhere in the hope of a fresh start and a better life.

The family left Warracknabeal after the devastating Federation Drought in the early 1900s and walked their horses and wagon with their selected possessions and six children to either Portland or Melbourne (some 366 km), where they loaded everything on board a ship — including the horses and wagon — which then sailed to Albany. Once they arrived there, they unloaded and walked it all to Narrogin (nearly another 300km). The amazing Ede went on to have another four children at the family's first WA camp called Highfield.

*Cliff Parsons aged two in Warracknabeal 1907*

# Emily Edith Bland

Emily Edith 'Ede' Bland was the daughter of Henry Joseph William (Joseph), born in Bedfordshire England and Emily Bland (née Mann), born in Geelong, Victoria. When Ede's father Joseph, was aged two, he and his family left England on the ship Caroline Agnes. Joseph's parents must have been desperate to risk the lives of their three small children aboard ship.

*Unfortunately, the journey did not go well for everyone in Joseph's family. Joseph had an older brother called James, who was four, and another brother called Ebenezer Alexander, who sadly died at sea during the trip. James and Harriet Bland and their two surviving sons arrived in Australia in June 1849. The very same year Ede's mother, Emily Mann was born in Geelong.*

*George and his sons Les and Stan at work on Highfield in 1910*

*George Parsons and 'Valcourt', his two-year-old prize winner Draught horse at Highfield, Narrogin 1910*

Joseph Bland's parents went directly to Geelong where they had another son, called Ephraim, in 1851. Many years later Joseph Bland Jnr met and married Emily Mann in Geelong. Their first child Emily Edith (known as Ede), was also born in Geelong. It is unclear at this stage how the Blands came to be in Minyip. But what is clear, is that five of their seven children, were born in or around Minyip:

*Edith Emily (Ede), b. Ceres 1872 reg 1316*
*Lillian Evelyn, b. Ceres 1874 reg 1202*
*Mary Ann, b. Horsham 1876 reg 10012*
*Bertha Amy, b. Minyip 1878 reg 10487*
*Walter Henry, b. Minyip 1880 reg 23939*
*Charles Oliver, b. Minyip 1883 reg 4151*
*Laura Isabella, b. Minyip 1885 reg 4591*

*Walter Henry, b. Minyip 1880 reg 23939*
*Charles Oliver, b. Minyip 1883 reg 4151*
*Laura Isabella, b. Minyip 1885 reg 4591*

Ede Bland was 22 when she married George F. Parsons Jnr (who was 23). Together they had six children in Victoria. There is proof they owned land west of Beulah, and also made their mark in Whitton Lakes area just out of Warracknabeal. It seems probable they may have lived at Sheep Hills homestead alongside George's parents.

As discussed in Chapter One, the hardship caused by the 1894-1904 Federation Drought was challenging to everyone. Nonetheless, Minyip appeared to be the place to be. It was the home of Australian agronomist William Farrer (b.1845, d.1906), a plant breeder best remembered for his Federation strain of wheat. The strain resulted in better quality and yields for the Australian wheat harvest. He is now known as the father of the Australian wheat industry.

All this experience and influence was well absorbed by George F. Parsons Jnr, whose farming expertise in their new home of Highfield in Narrogin, WA, was much sought after and respected for years to come.

Even though Ede's parentage was Victorian, it appears her parents and siblings also came to live in Narrogin. It is not clear how or when they arrived, but it may have been associated with the trying conditions. The drought had come hot on the heels of devastating floods and plagues of rabbits in addition to the disruptive carving-up of the large land runs in the early 1900s. This made way for smaller land holdings.

# The lure of Western Australia

People in eastern Australia became very aware of Western Australia in the run up to Federation in 1901. WA refused to get involved in Federation issues and even considered maintaining complete independence. The Kalgoorlie-Boulder gold rush, although slowing, highlighted the potential wealth the state offered. The Western Australian government certainly targeted the folk who had lost their way in the declining gold industry of the Eastern Goldfields, with the lure of potential wealth from wheat farming.

Western Australian wheat commanded competitive prices overseas. According to Associate Professor Andrea Gaynor, from the Centre for Western Australian History at the University of WA, *The West Australian Settler's Guide and Farmer's Handbook* showed great optimism, with the promise of 'cheap land, railways, credit and subsidised conditional immigration'.

Looking at a map, it appears a simple feat to board a ship and sail from Melbourne to Albany, but sailing across the Great Australian Bight was not for the faint-hearted. Even today, sailors treat that area with enormous respect, often preferring to sail around the top of Australia instead. But with news of a railway line being laid between Albany and Perth, it was a very attractive option.

In the late 1890s, with the Great Southern Railway Line being built from Albany to Perth, the government opened up new land opportunities around Narrogin. The Narrogin area had a water supply, which allowed for a mid-way rail stop, and the town emerged in the early 1900s. Not only did the smaller holdings on offer prove attractive to settlers from the eastern states, but also failing and struggling gold prospectors were in the mix.

No doubt people were attracted by having tenure over the land, on the proviso they cleared it and paid what could be considered as a small annual rental. The new settlers made short work of the local wild life, both for the cash back for the pelts and to remove competition for the pasture and crops. This began to affect the local and traditional food source for the Aboriginal tribes in the area.

Sadly, as more people arrived, the Aboriginal tribes were pushed into delegated camps. Because the new settlers came from hardships of their own, very little was done to ease the plight of the Noongar people.

Alan remembers his grandfather providing work to one particular Aboriginal man, but for the most part, the 'White Australia' Policy implemented by the federal government had far reaching effects on the treatment of Aboriginal people.

Some settlers and Aboriginal people found an income stripping bark from the Brown Mallet trees in the area, at least until it was restricted in the 1920s. Mallet bark contained high quality, water-soluble tannins, used in the production of quality leather (Anna Haebich, *For Their Own Good*). This is supported in a document produced by the *Heritage Council* in 2009:

> *European settlement in the Williams-Narrogin area began in the 1860s, when pastoral leases were made available. This was followed by closer settlement associated with village leases. Many new settlers needed capital to develop farms, so began harvesting mallet for the high-quality tannin found in the bark. By the early 1900s a sizeable tannin industry had become established in the area. Dryandra was originally dedicated as State forest in 1903, as an area for the protection of water catchments and growing wandoo and mallet forests. Many of the early pioneers arrived with their families and possessions on buggies and carts. Some selections had a small hut while others had nothing at all. Often the decision was made to set up house some distance away from a water source, for fear of flooding, which may explain why many early Narrogin homesteads ended up a mile or so from water.*

The Department of Agriculture document, by Mollemans and Beeston, 1992, *Distribution and ecological significance of on-farm bushland remnants in southern wheatbelt region of Western Australia* states that:

*Highfield Farm, Narrogin in the 1920s*

*The area around Narrogin contained medium-height trees with an incomplete canopy more open than a forest. Areas of Mallee and Salt Bush etc. provided low wooded scrub. With a freshwater lake in the area clearing the land would not have been too arduous.*

*Indeed, effective land clearing techniques were developed quickly. The timber from a felled tree was cut and stacked in a trench dug around the stump. Fires could be set alight after February through until the following summer. The heat from the fire would make short work of most of the stump and the land could be prepared for cultivation.*

According to Associate Professor Andrea Gaynor, a government whose greatest intent was to clear the land to plant grains, thus achieving employment and the promise of prosperity, lured many people. No consideration was given to the nutrient value of cleared land. To achieve their goal, the WA Government subsidised settlement, making land clearing a conditional requirement. But Gaynor says 'the Wheatbelt was never self-sustaining'.

The original pastoralists in the State sensibly managed large holdings of virgin bush, which did not disturb the wildlife and First Peoples too much. In the early 1900s, the land was carved up into small packages. Firstly, around the railways and good fertile acreages, then as demand increased, they began carving up the land into packages of percentages of good, not so good, and outright poisonous land. These latter lots were often remote. However, the Government carved up the land anyway, then apparently poured money into failing properties with the establishment of the Industries Assistance Board. As Gaynor writes in her essay, How to eat a Wilderness:

*Development therefore occurred over widely scattered areas, producing isolated farms and small dispersed communities. This pattern arguably increased settler vulnerability to economic and psychological hardship.*

There is evidence George and his family were probably in the second wave of settlers. However, as yet, there is no evidence of the Bland family's arrival, except for the name of their property, which was found in a 1925 WA Government Gazette. According to the Gazette, the name of Joseph Bland's property was 'Eden Valley'.

*Joseph and Emily Bland 1920s*

*Front: Joseph and Emily Bland with great-granddaughter Audrey, aged 4*
*Back: Ede Parsons with son Les, father of Audrey Parsons, 1921*

As a child, Alan remembers the Bland farmhouse next to the road out of Narrogin about four or five miles (seven kilometres) on the Corrigin road. Ede's father, Joseph, was a memorable character — especially to four-year-old Alan. His great-grandfather wore a waistcoat and sported a long white beard the full length of the waistcoat (to his navel). He may have even started to grow it the day this photograph was taken. The wearing of a waistcoat is of consequence as it tells today's generation that despite the unusually long beard, he considered himself a gentleman. Emily, his wife, maintained the standard and always dressed like a fine lady with a frilled high-necked blouse, bodice and long skirt. Although the long skirt would have been long out dated, she still held her dignity.

## *Developing Narrogin*

Extracted from *Noman's Lake — a collection of memories*,
by Heidi Astbury and Lyn Chadwick, 1987:

> *In 1898 the Homestead Act was passed which allowed the pastoral lease holders the option of claiming the farmland around the homestead. (A homestead site of 160 acres was allowed, this could then be extended at a later date to complete the farm.) The region in the vicinity of Noman's Lake was surveyed for land settlement and farming in the period 1904 – 1907 (S13 P.W.D. Plan 12064 1905 – 1907).*

*The Parsons and Bland families in Narrogin c.1920s*

The Narrogin area was home to many dingoes when the Bland and Parsons families arrived. The cunning dingo made short work of many a settler's livestock as they enjoyed feasting on poultry and sheep, seemingly kept just for them in the fenced confines. Even though the dingo was indigenous, they were considered vermin and the government put a bounty on their scalps to encourage settlers to kill them and collect the cash. Many kangaroos frequented the area and some farmers kept kangaroo dogs, which would chase down the roos and kill them. Kangaroo shooting was also encouraged as the skins could be sold. Possum pelts were considered a very saleable item and a few enterprising settlers caught possums in snares for this very reason. Such pastimes gave the new settlers a much-needed cash flow for supplies. But it was the 'Underground Mutton' which reliably sustained both Aboriginal and settler alike. With nine children to feed, it was probable that both the Parsons and the Bland families succeeded at some form of hunting for food and sale of pelts.

The Narrogin Shire describes the town at the time the Bland and Parsons families were in the district:

*Narrogin was one of the largest towns on the fringe of the Wheatbelt region. It had two hotels, two boarding-houses, two shops, a doctor, a chemist and a small hospital on a hill away from the railway station. It was on the Great Southern Railway Line and a train went through once a day from Perth to Albany.*

George and Ede's grandson, Alan Parsons, remembers Ede as always feeding a large extended family. To do this she had to rise early to milk the cow, then light the fire before making a large breakfast consisting of a huge pot of porridge, followed by a whopping pile of boiled eggs alongside a mountain of toast and hot tea in a vast teapot. Come morning tea time, she made a mammoth batch of scones and another large pot of tea, which she took out to anyone working in the paddocks.

n 1926 George and Ede set off to cross the little-travelled Nullarbor Plain. Ede meticulously kept a journal (see Appendix II).

*George and Ede Parsons amongst the fruit trees in their garden in the 1920s*

Leader in farming technology

*Bagging chaff at Highfield, 1920s*

The Narrogin settlers' community on the whole showed great willingness to support each other in various clearing and farming progressions, with everyone chipping in to help on their properties when required. Many people came from unimaginable difficulties with next to nothing and just had to make do. One such family were the Carnegies. They had come from a potato famine in Ireland, to what seemed like a dream come true until reality had its way. Charlie, his pregnant wife, and three children arrived in Narrogin at around the same time as the Parsons, only Charlie's path was immediately shadowed in grief. His wife died in childbirth leaving the family lost and confused. George offered Charlie work and Ede took his three children under her wing. Later the children also worked on Highfield, before leaving for a life in Perth. Charlie's continuing loyalty to George and Ede, in appreciation of this gesture was unfailing.

*George Parsons and Bert Ponsford at Highfield,1928. One of Charlie Carnegie's daughters married Bert Ponsford, manager of Perth's Embassy Ballroom*

George Frederick Parsons is on the Shire of Narrogin's Honour Board for the Narrogin Road Board 1892-1961, for his significant ten-year contribution, between 1915-1925, which included the position as Chairman from 1923-1925.

*Parsons siblings: Cliff, Ella, Stan, and Bert, 1928*

Highfield was about five kilometres out of Narrogin. As teenagers, the young Parsons mob would walk into town for socialising and especially for the dances known as 'Balls'. Eva and Maud, the two younger daughters, were little terrors who, although forbidden to go to town, hid dresses under the bridge down the road. They would go to bed as normal then steal away into the night to the bridge where they would don their fancy frocks and head off into town to a prohibited dance.

*Young Eva and Maude Parsons, aged 11 and 9, on horseback, 1924*

A young Cliff (Alan's Father) and a few of his mates would regularly go into town on a Saturday night. They watched a bachelor farmer who took his horse and sulky into town every Saturday, tie it up and then head off to the pub for a day's heavy drinking. Come night, he would stagger out, find the sulky, point the horse to home, collapsing into the sulky seat to leave the horse to find its own way back to his farm.

Cliff and his mates decided to play a trick on this chap. They unharnessed the horse from the sulky, pushed the shafts of the sulky through the fence then walked the horse to the gate leading into the paddock and back down to the shafts on that side of the fence and harnessed him up again. The next morning, the flummoxed farmer was found sound asleep in the sulky where it stood.

## Cliff meets Alma

Cliff met Alma Muir in Narrogin, in the mid-to-late 1920s. They married in 1928, and Alan was born there on 12 February 1929. Hardship began almost immediately, with Cliff's constant search for work, which took the young family to live first with Cliff's parents on the family farm, Highfield, and then onto wherever further work pursuits took them, but more about that later.

Alma Parsons, née Shannon (Muir), as young woman in 1925

Cliff Parsons in Narrogin, 1926

## Short backstory about Alma Muir, Alan's mother

Alan's mother Alma was the first child of five children born to Alf and Louise Muir. The family lived in Collie. Alma's birth date is 14 March 1905. As a small girl, she was given to Alice and Jack Shannon, although no paperwork was ever produced.

Alice Shannon, (b. Muir), Alf Muir's sister, was unable to have children, so Alf and his wife Louise happily gave their first born, Alma, to the Shannons. Alice and Jack raised Alma until she was 18-years-old.

Leader in farming technology    63

*Baby Alma in Collie, 1906*

Jack Shannon was the Station Master in Narrogin so Alma went to live there with her foster parents. Jack and Alice Shannon thought very highly of Alma, believing her to be a 'good girl'. As a young woman in Narrogin, Alma experienced some brief amateur theatrical involvement and enjoyed a pleasant social life.

*Alma Muir aged five*

*Narrogin Theatre 1920s, Alma Muir is second from the left in the front row*

In between time, she readily cared for unwell or elderly relatives. By the time Alma was 18, life in rural Australia began to change. Australia was still recovering from the devastating results of World War I and the loss of thousands of young men in rural communities. A few years later, in the western world at large, an imminent Depression loomed along with a pending second World War. But glazed in hope and romance and just before these world events took hold, Alma accepted a proposal of marriage from Clifford Parsons. They were married on 15 February 1928 but Alma came to experience difficulties in her married life, and although she overcame them it was a source of sadness for the Shannon's.

## *The Nullarbor Crossing*

Two years before Alma and Cliff's wedding, George and Ede made the unusual decision to return to Warracknabeal by a six cylinder Austin automobile in 1926. At the time the artery across the Nullarbor Plain was not a road but a track, sometimes with long grass obscuring any signs of wheel imprints to follow. In places tracks were either rough and sandy and full of wombat burrows or very rocky and apt to cause punctures. Once you left the telegraph poles in WA you needed to have your compass at the ready.

When the Austin left Norseman in WA it was 900 miles before the next town in SA. Stations were hundreds of miles apart. In 1926 the Nullarbor might have revealed a lone linesman travelling in a buggy pulled by two camels, or the odd camel team hauling bails of wool from the stations. Wild life and the occasional sighting of a tribe of aboriginal people would also engage the intrepid traveller (see Appendix II).

## *Highfield lost*

When Alan was three, George and Ede's second eldest son, Fred, arrived home with some devastating news. Fred, an experienced playboy, a gambler and an alcoholic, had bought a farm up near Bruce Rock, for which his father had guaranteed Fred's loan through the bank. However, the upshot of this act of trusting kindness abruptly spiralled out of control when Fred finally went bankrupt, and George and Ede lost their much-loved farming property, Highfield. This put an end to all the hard work invested in building up, and creating, the family's heritage and their place in the community.

After more than twenty years of contribution to the community, George Parsons was so well-liked and respected by the townsfolk of Narrogin, that when the bank foreclosed on his farm in about 1932, the town made them Freemen of Narrogin. The Shire presented him with a tall grandfather clock (which tick-tocked and chimed away in Cliff and Alma's Dalkeith house all through the '60s). The clock went to Brian, Alan's younger brother, who was still a farmer in Corrigin when Cliff died.

*George Parsons seated centre with his sons Les on the left and Fred on the right.
Rear, from left, Stan, Cliff and Bert, 1920*

Their neighbours, the Treforts, who lived next to Highfield, bought the property. (Alan recalls in the late '60s being on the Cuballing Road and coming across them — noting they had turned the property into an abattoir)

## Back to the 1930s

Unfortunately, it was the start of The Great Depression and things were really tough, with rampant unemployment and depressed prices for goods. Alan remembers:

*Men would walk onto the farm and offer to do any sort of work, for a meal or a few shillings then walk on to the next farm. I can remember that situation happening many times. They were known as tramps; their only possessions being what they could carry. Many farmers walked off their farms, as they could not handle any debts or bank loans. That was how George Parsons got to manage the farm 'Emoh Ruo'. The farmer was forced off by the Finance Co, who then employed suitable people to manage the farm, do all the work and grow their own food. I do not know how they were paid to do cropping etc. Expenses would accrue.*

However, good fortune soon followed the highly respected George, and he was offered a job by a finance company called National Assurance, who appointed managers to take over their repossessed properties. They offered George and his sons management of a farm east of Corrigin, at Bendering. Alan rightly wondered about how the managers were paid to do their cropping. It now comes to light that there were government subsidies available and no doubt the finance company either directed, or procured, these subsidies for their farm managers.

The property was called Emoh Ruo, 'Our Home' spelt backwards. George, with the help of his family, successfully managed the property for many years and it was looked upon as the family's new home. Old Charlie Carnegie had followed George and Edith to Emoh Ruo, where he lived in a humpy, but always ate his meals with the family at the main dinner table. As the now adult Parsons boys branched out to their own properties or ventures, Charlie was there for them too. It is said he was more than willing to do all the dirty odd jobs, perhaps because once he was on the age pension he was paid in cash in hand. In those days work on the farm was plentiful, especially as six horses were needed to pull a three-furrow plough through the heavy clay soils in Corrigin. Horses were everything to the farmer, except when you had a tricycle!

With all the men folk in the Parsons' clan hard at work on the Corrigin property, a young Alan recalls, with fascination, his mother's extraordinary efforts to fix his tricycle. Alan, apparently already savvy with mechanical engineering, knew something was wrong with the final fixed result but was unable to influence his well-intentioned mother, and thereupon was assigned a tricycle with synchronized functioning pedals positioned exactly next to one another.

Alan says of his mother, 'She was not at all mechanical'.

*Alan Parsons, aged four, with his first truck, 1933*

# Part Two

## On surviving in Western Australia: Alan's life takes shape

Alan on his beloved bike alongside Cliff's International truck with Cliff squatting and Brian on the truck step Merredin 1939

*Alan, aged seven and Brian, aged 20 months, 1936*

CHAPTER THREE

# *"My grandfather always admired hard workers"*
## *Alan Parsons*

### *The relations and the stutter*

The year young Alan turned five his brother Brian was born, on the 7th of June 1934, at the height of the Great Depression. There was not enough income for all the family to work on Emoh Ruo, so it was very good fortune that Cliff and his family were given an opportunity by Alma's Uncle Shannon (her foster father); Jack Shannon was Station Master at Subiaco, and could get Cliff a job at the goods sheds in Perth.

In 1935, Alma, Cliff and the boys moved to Daglish, a suburb on the Fremantle train line in Perth. Alan attended his first school at Subiaco Primary. However, this was short lived. They stayed less than a year before Cliff found himself following work on the Wellington Dam Project near Collie. A deal was secured, which was only valid if Cliff bought a Bedford truck from a bloke called Syd Wheatley at Attwood Motors. Alan claims he never understood how his father paid for the truck but suspects his Great Uncle Shannon went guarantor for the payments. Owning a truck during those tough times certainly increased the likelihood of securing more work opportunities.

(On another note, serendipity played a hand as the tide of time turned. Syd was the father of a future business associate of a mature Alan, named Vern Wheatley, of the Automotive Holdings Group, with whom Alan was to do significant business in 1980s and '90s).

With the security of work and the family now living in Collie, they rented a house for about eighteen months, just across the road from the Muir's, Alma's birth family.

*Alma Parsons with her second son Brian in 1934*

## *The abscess and the comics*

In 1936, when Alan was seven and still in Collie, he suffered an abscess in his ear and was put in Collie Hospital, but they could not do anything for him there. His parents arrived at the hospital in Uncle Bert's car. So, his dad borrowed Bert's car because it had wind up windows, which would help keep Alan warm and therefore his level of pain down during the long trip ahead to Perth and Royal Perth Hospital. Alan was left at the hospital all by himself — but not before his dad had gone out and bought him a big pile of comics, indeed a one-off and memorable gesture. Alan stayed there for six long and lonely weeks. When he was well again, Alan returned to Collie.

*Alan Parsons aged 8, riding Teddy in 1937 on a holiday visit to his grandparents at Emoh Ruo in Corrigin*

However, when the Wellington Dam job finished in 1938, Cliff and Alma had to return to Corrigin with four-year-old Brian, leaving the school-aged Alan with the Muirs so that he could continue his education. This seemingly harsh decision was made simply because there weren't any schools where his parents and little brother were going.

It turned out Alan was left-handed. Unfortunately, in those days, this was looked upon as an affliction to be corrected. The teachers, therefore, set about forcing him to write with his right hand; a practice now widely acknowledged as traumatising and interfering with the nervous pathways in a child's brain, sometimes resulting in a stutter. Alan, like any child, was no doubt also disturbed by his parents leaving him, albeit in the hands of family he knew. To top things off, one day, when walking home from school a bigger boy beat little Alan up. It wasn't long before a bewildered Alan began to stutter.

## *The Muir family*

With Alan's parents and his little brother Brian now living in Corrigin for several months at a time, and Alan attending school whilst living with Alma's birth parents in Collie, it could be argued Alan learnt a great deal by participating in the lives of his ever-inventive uncles and grandfather Muir. These men left no stone unturned when applying themselves to life's challenges during the tail end of the Great Depression. Their solutions to mechanical problems were nothing short of ingenious, supporting the belief that 'anything is possible'.

Alma's siblings were Alan's Uncles, Bert and Keith, and Aunts, Gladys and Jean. Alma was first born followed by Gladys, [Al]Bert, Keith then Jean.

Times were still difficult due to the Depression and the threat of another war, but, being resourceful folk, the Muir family managed to maintain life in a big house with a tennis court. Alan describes their set up in the town of Collie:

Bert (2yrs), Alma (6 yrs), and Gladys (4 yrs) Muir, photographed in Ballarat Victoria, 1911

*The Muir Family: Keith front left; Jean, a friend, Gladys behind, Alma in centre, Bert, with parents Louise and Alf Muir at rear*

*Their property in Jones Street consisted of a house with a tennis court and a sawmill through to Keith's house, which fronted Robert Street. There was also a garage which housed two trucks, a bus, two cars and other gear. Muir's address was Roberts Street. My family first rented the house on the opposite side of the road in Jones Street; Keith and Elise were also facing Jones Street as the block went right through, so Keith and Elise were next to the sawmill and garage. It was good fun for a little boy.*

At the time of Alan's schooling in Collie, Keith had already married Elise Pearce at Wellington Mills on 26 February 1935. Their eldest son Darryl was born in 1936, followed by Jon. However, in 1938 when nine-year-old Alan arrived at the Muir household, Darryl was just two-years-old.

Alma's grandparents, Alf (Albert Ernest) Muir b.1878-1959, and Louise (Elizabeth Louisa née Bolton) b.1884-1972, arrived in Collie in 1904, the year before Alma was born. It seems they had met in Perth and were married in Subiaco during 1904. Alf Muir was born in Victoria to William Muir and Ada Joans somewhere in the Castlemaine area.

William Muir was a Scott, and, according to family memory, was more than likely lured to Australia along with his family in the 1850s. However, as the shorelines were awash with men by that name, many of them looking for gold, it is difficult to pinpoint where his parents settled, possibly at Barkers Creek, or near Castlemaine.

It is not clear how or why Alf Muir, aged 22, was in Perth, WA, but what is known is that he had worked on the WA Railways since February 1900. He began his work in Perth city as a lamp man and a porter. In 1901 he was promoted, learning to become a shunter on the Fremantle goods trains. Between 1904 and 1910, after his marriage to Louise, he was transferred to Collie where he worked as a train guard.

During the early 1900s, WA leant heavily on the railways to assist opening up the inland regions. Coal and water were the fuels used for the steam engines, both of which were plentiful in Collie. According to the railway history of the Collie River Valley area, this lead to Collie being the second largest rail centre in the State after Fremantle.

Along with the State's enthusiasm for Collie's abundance of coal and water was it's fervour for the abundance of jarrah forests, as explained on the Collie River Valley website:

> *Also essential in building the rail network were wooden sleepers over which the railway tracks were laid. Again, Collie with its large jarrah forests provided hundreds of thousands of railway sleepers. Timber mills were plentiful, with some such as Worsley and Lyall's Mill supporting communities into the 1950s.*

Alf Muir appeared to have landed in heaven, and very quickly created a saw mill as well as establishing himself in a number of other capacities, in order to be part of the rapid development. It may be that Alf was possibly better suited to self-employment since his railway work record was dotted with reprimands and docked pays, with some underlying mentions of missing items. The last entry seems to imply the railway authorities thought he'd intentionally lost a bundle of iron...which may have led to his departure. The following is from the work record: *'CAUTIONED. ONE BUNDLE IRON MISSING. 21-6-1910'.*

Over the years, Alf (Pop) Muir ran a carrier truck service, worked in the mines, had a sawmill and ran a small farm. The farm was just out of town on Williams Road. Alan remembers going out to the farm with him for a couple of weekend stays and recognising it was his hideaway.

*Alf Muir (with pipe), wife Louise Muir and children, Bert and Jean c.1920*

Alan's Auntie Gladys married Ray Piper and had two children, Rayesy and Neil, but Gladys, for reasons of her own, divorced Ray while he was overseas at the war. She then married a taxi driver called Lou King with whom she had one child called Lyle.

When Alan's Uncle Bert lived in Collie, he had a girlfriend called Mac for a number of years. But when Bert was called up during WWII it seems things changed. When he returned home after the war he left Collie to work as the green keeper at the bowling club in Geraldton and married a young woman called Margaret Patricia

*Gladys Muir in harlequin costume c.1930*

*Keith and Elise Muir, Collie c.1935*

Foley in 1946, and together they had a son, Colin (b.1950, d.2003). There was some mention that they lived for a time in Kalgoorlie. Alan recalls visiting the little family when Bert retired to Midland in the 1950s. He remembers Bert's wife as 'stand-offish', and that Bert was the father of a son just three years older than his eldest daughter.

Keith started a truck business. As previously mentioned, owning a truck increased your work options, and an astute Keith quickly found a niche collecting bottles, batteries, scrap metal and other recyclable materials. In 1942, during the war years, Keith, his wife Elise and their children, moved to Mandurah. The family lived alongside Elise's parents, Charles and Amy (née Foster) Pearce, in a small flat on their property in Tuckey St. Keith was then able to join the Royal Australian Air Force.

*Keith and Elise Muir, with their sons, from the left Jon and Darryl with their adopted daughter Donnelle in front of Elise, Mandurah c1940s.*

When he returned from the war, Keith built up a very successful business using his ingenuity and following the needs of the people and trends in industry. During this period, he and Alan worked with one another trucking wheat in the Wheatbelt. Keith always made the most of these trips and loaded various collected items on his return journey. The family soon moved to their own home at 7 Davey Street, Mandurah.

Keith began to clean the used motor oil he collected, and thereby began a very lucrative business. His equally capable son, Darryl, took over the business and was able to provide his family with a life of relative luxury.

Alan says his Aunty Jean was referred to as a rebel. She married a Shell truck driver called Bill Williamson but, unfortunately, Bill was an alcoholic. The marriage did not last and tragically, Jean ended up an alcoholic herself and died at a very early age.

Jean Muir in Collie c.1930

When Alan lived with the Muirs, his Uncle Bert took Alan under his wing and taught him how to ride a bike on the home tennis court and how to box on the back veranda, buying Alan a set of boxing gloves.

Bert was unmarried at the time, and for business reasons, he still lived at home with his parents. Bert had a truck and bus business which gave him work, transporting miners to and from the Collie mine site. Sometimes Alan, aged between seven and nine, would go on the bus. These trips became special times for Alan since he was proudly fussed over. Alan's relationship with his Muir uncles was always fruitful and, remarkably, continued into Alan's own working life, with the first working association formed when Alan was fifteen and then continued on and off into the 1970s.

## *Muir family tree*

Many Scottish surnames refer to the topographic area from where the person lived, thus Muir is the name used for someone who lived beside a moor.

The Scots were encouraged to migrate to Victoria prior to, and during, the gold rush days of the early 1850s. The situation in Scotland had changed for both farmers and town dwellers in the mid-18th century, as the industrial age took its toll and unavoidable changes rolled in. Farmers (crofters) in the Highlands were pushed off their small farms to make way for larger holdings, enabling more sheep to be run for greater profit. The few small crofters who hung on to their land, then suffered the devastation of the Highland Potato Famine (1846-57), a crop on which they had previously survived. Meanwhile, in the towns, steam driven industries soon created unbearable living and working conditions, all the while squeezing out the once flourishing cottage industry and working class.

**Albert Ernest Muir (Alf)** b. 9th February 1878, d.1959 Mosman Park (b. in Victoria to William Muir and Ada Jones) Married in Subiaco in 1904 to Elizabeth Louisa Bolton (Louise) b.1884, d.1972, Mosman Park

**Alma Muir** b. 14 March 1905 in Collie, d. 28 October 1977 in Perth
Married in Narrogin 1928 to Clifford Parsons b. 4th Nov 1905 in Warracknabeal, Victoria, d.21 July 1984 in Spearwood, Perth. Children: Alan b.12 February 1929, Brian b. 7th June 1934

**Gladys Muir** b.1907 Collie, d.1973 in Bicton, Perth. Married 1926 to Raymond Piper (divorced) Married 1946 to Lou King. Children: Lyle b.1947

**Albert Muir** b.1909 Collie, d.2002 Midland. Married 1946 to Margaret Patricia Foley Children: Colin Muir b.1950, d.2003, East Fremantle

**Keith Muir** b. 4th January 1914 in Collie, d. 23 May 2003, Sorrento, WA
Married at Wellington 26 February 1935 to Elise Pearce b. 29 August 1912 Collie, d. 4th September 1994, Sorrento, WA. Children: Darryl b.13 August 1936, Jon b.17 July1941, Donnelle Kerry b. 6th August 1947 (adopted daughter, birth name Marie Harrower)

**Jean Muir** b.1916, Collie, d. 1977, registered Katanning, WA
Married 1936 in Collie to William (Bill) Williamson, divorced. Married 1954 to Leonard Hunt, (previously married to Dora) lived in Dumbleyung with Jean, d 1972

## *Merredin*

At long last, when Alan was nearly ten-years-old, his parents decided he could once again return to live with them in their new home in Merredin. It was 1939 and World War II had broken out, leading to the continuation of uncertain times. Alan remembers the difficult trip from Collie to Merredin. The Muirs put him on the train in Collie, which travelled to Wagin and Narrogin, finally arriving in Corrigin. Alan continued the trip from there to Merredin on the back of his father's truck.

As petrol rationing was a reality, people found travel difficult and did not venture far. Alan's father, Cliff, was fortunate to have obtained a trucking job as a contractor with the railways in the construction of the line from Merredin to Kalgoorlie.

However, as Cliff would only be home on Wednesdays and weekends, this left Alma to raise and care for the two boys on her own. Thrust into isolation, far from family support, Alma had a difficult time coping with the gruelling domestic chores and raising her young sons, ten-year-old Alan and five-year-old Brian. Although Alma was proficient at caring for others (with a solid track record of caring for sick and dying relatives most of her formative years), she found she was overwhelmed and not able to apply herself to the required practical and arduous ways of the bush.

Brian and Alan ready for school in Merredin 1939. Due to financial difficulties Alan wore these same boots for many years causing his growing feet to deform

Alan says he enjoyed his schooling experience in Merredin. When asked why, he explained it was because he was back with his family and that, with his father away most of the week, he felt strong in his role as the man of the house. He also got a job with the local newsagent delivering papers after school, using his bike to ride some sixteen miles to do so.

The journey over rough roads, with the papers carried over the bar, was littered with double-gees, a long-pronged prickle, which could penetrate and flatten a bicycle tyre tube in seconds. It got so that Alan could patch and repair a puncture in ten minutes whilst on the job.

Nonetheless, the family could ill afford luxury items like new boots, so because his fast-growing trotters were forced every day into tight leather boots, Alan's feet began to change shape. The arch curved higher and higher to accommodate and allow the ball of his foot and toes the facility to grip when on the move. Regrettably, once shaped this way, his feet never returned to their intended form.

Whilst living in Merredin, Alan suffered a painful whitlow finger. He had already endured the excruciating throbbing infection for a week, when the family decided to go on a weekend trip to stay with his grandparents, on Cliff's side, in Corrigin. At that stage, the only mode of transport was Cliff's truck. Even though Alan was in agony, his parents could not let him ride in the cab out of the wind because the front of the truck was too small and Brian was too young to take Alan's place on the tray at the back. He had to travel two hours over many bumpy miles on the tray, requiring him to hang on tightly. To top it off, the weather was bad all the way from Merredin to Corrigin. Having survived the harrowing trip there, Alan remembers only too well the excruciating pain suffered in the freezing cold night air on the return trip.

Two days later, Alan rode his bike to the Merredin hospital to have the whitlow lanced and, after recovering from the chloroform anaesthetic but still wobbly, he rode his bike home again. As life progressed into the 1940s Alan says:

*When the war started in 1939, everything changed again. Men joined the services and rationing was introduced. Farmers were restricted from joining up as food had to be produced, which is why none of the Parsons men were called up.*

*When the war ended in 1945, service men started to come home, looking for jobs in order to get back on their feet. There were huge shortages of everything. Rationing kept going for another two or three years. Many returned servicemen were wrecks, physically and mentally. A lot of broken marriages, suicides also began to occur.*

## The truck

Uncle Bert (Muir) had converted his bus to a tray-top truck, with a wooden cab without doors. Over time, Cliff was able to purchase this truck for £50, a very reasonable sum in those days. When the opportunity came, Alan, aged twelve, used the very same truck to learn to drive a loaded vehicle. Alan used the truck for farm work and from the age of fifteen he carted all his father's wheat by himself.

The truck itself was a single wheel, 30 cwt, with which he carted about 36 bags at any one time, amounting to over three tons. The war was still on, so blowing a tyre was out of the question because a replacement was almost impossible to locate. Consequently, Alan had to develop exceptional driving skills over the corrugations, to avoid both his father's wrath and the possible collapse of his own fledgling business as a wheat carter.

Petrol rationing created problems with an allocation of just five gallons per month. The truck, which was created from a converted bus, had an English Morris Commercial motor, running on petrol. Alan cleverly changed it over to run on kerosene so that he could achieve five or six carting trips a day, instead of per month. He also tried to get into town early to be first on the weighbridge each morning to achieve the maximum amount of loads that day.

*George Parsons with his daughters Eva, Maude and Ella, all strong women, at Emoh Ruo, late 1930s*

## *Meanwhile what was happening to George and Edith?*

Alan's paternal grandparents had also faced some challenges. Edith (Ede), who worked very hard all her life, had always maintained a home that everyone seemed to want to visit and/or stay awhile. At Emoh Ruo, as at Highfield, she, of course, continued to do all the cooking and cleaning as well as other outdoors duties.

When the lease on the Emoh Ruo farm ended in the late 1930s, they moved into Corrigin. Here they took on the lease of the town's hostel, which served as accommodation for many single men working in and around the district. Once again, Edith tackled all of the onerous domestic tasks whilst catering to the requirements for all who boarded there. Her cooking, laundry and cleaning duties magnified, seeing her working even harder. Ivy and Maude, their oldest and youngest daughters, also lived at the hostel. Maude had a wind-up gramophone, which Alan, aged about eleven, loved to experience when he went there. Grandad George Parsons did all the yard duties, chopping wood, etc. He also did a great deal of voluntary work around town, which earned him great respect.

# *On the move, again*

Finally, Cliff's contract with the railways in Merredin finished, and in 1940, he was financially able to lease a farm, in Kunjin, east of Corrigin. Alan was aged eleven when the family leased this farm from Wattie Hewitt and moved there. The lease was £175 per annum, including sheep and farm machinery. Alma's struggles and sufferance of undue stress, far from family support, had ended and life began to offer some stability.

The ups and downs of farming life began almost immediately. Believing the newly invented tractors were the future in farming, Cliff sold his truck and purchased a tractor. However, things turned bad when diesel crude oil was rumoured to be running out — Cliff immediately sold the tractor and bought a team of horses. This action affected Alan's chores, which were already plentiful and variable according to the seasons, because from then on, they always included feeding the stable of nine or so horses, late at night. Cliff also kept a fine horse for riding to and from various destinations.

Alan and Brian both used a horse and sulky to go four miles to the Kunjin school for a year or more. Upon arrival, they would unharness the horse from the sulky then tie the animal up to a tree and feed it a bag of chaff. The boys repeated the harnessing procedure to get home again after school. Whilst Alan and Brian attended Kunjin School, there was just one teacher for the fifteen pupils present. Despite being in school, Alan was asked to work from correspondence lessons, making his schooling again a disjointed experience.

*Cliff Parsons cutting hay with a team of horses in the 1940s*

# *A home of their own for Alan's grandparents*

As their age progressed, George and Edith moved to a beautiful and spacious house next to the Corrigin Town Hall. However, it was not long before George passed away, on the 4th of May 1940. It was a very big funeral, with George being honoured as one of the town's highly respected pioneers. Alan says of the day, 'the eleven grandchildren were sent to play on the Corrigin Rock while the funeral was held.'

*The grandchildren in 1940 — Alan is second from the right in the back row*
*Right to left: baby Robyn Hallett, held by Beryl Parsons, Lynn Parsons, Alan Parsons, Doug Parsons, John Hallett, Carlton Hallett, Colin Parsons, Neville Parsons, Brian Parsons, Phyllis Parsons*
*Absent: Ray, Les and Kaye Parsons. Audrey Parsons*

The following is from the death notices in The West Australian, 5th May 1940
(see Obituary in Appendix III):

PARSONS. In loving memory of
George Frederick, who passed
away May 4, 1940.
Sad and sudden was the parting.
Hard and cruel was the blow.
How sadly we have missed you
No one on earth will ever know,
We loved you then, we love you still,
Forget you Dad, we never will.

Inserted by his sorrowing wife and daughter Ede and Maud

PARSONS G. In loving memory of our
dear Father and Granddad,
who passed away May 4, 1940.
Not a day do we forget you.
In our hearts you are always near;
We who loved you sadly miss you.
As It ends this first sad year.

Inserted by his loving son and daughter in-law, Stan and Olive, and grandchildren, Beryl, Doug, Colln and Phyllis.

PARSONS. George Frederick. In loving
memory of our dear Father, who passed
away, suddenly, on May 4, 1940.
In silence we remember.

Inserted by his loving son and daughter-in-law, Fred and Mabel, and grandsons, Lynn and Neville

PARSONS. G. F. Loving memory of
our dear Dad and Grandpa, who
passed away May 4, 1940.
Ever remembered.

Inserted by his loving son and daughter-in law and grandson, Bert, Jean and Ray.

*George Frederick Parsons, early 1940*

PARSONS. Loving memory of our dear Daddy and Bamps who passed away May 4, 1940. So dearly loved, so sadly missed.

Inserted by his loving daughter Eva and son-in-law Tom, 'dad grandchildren, Carlton, John, and Robyn

PARSONS, G. F. In sad and loving memory of our beloved Father, who passed away May 4, 1940. Cherished- memories.

Inserted by his loving daughter and son-in-law, Ella and Wilfred.

Edith carried on living in their home for another couple of years. As it was a very big house, she continued to take in boarders to support herself and Ivy, their eldest daughter, who needed Edith's care throughout her life. Ivy was born without a mouth palate and could not speak, and was unable to conduct herself in society. She stayed close to her mother all through her childhood and most of her adult life.

Alan was sent to live with Edith, Maude and Ivy when George passed away, in order to help with the outside chores. As Alan was twelve, and there was still no such thing as a school bus in the area, this arrangement allowed Alan to continue his schooling in Corrigin. He rode his bike back to Kunjin every weekend to visit his family and work on his Dad's farm. The ride covered about twelve miles of dirt and corrugated road.

## *Alan dips his toes into the world of international business*

It was here in Corrigin that Alan, aged twelve, initially began his long business association with the International Harvester Company. Alan got his first job as the 'shit boy' with Weatherhead and Hill, the International Company in Corrigin. This after-school employment meant he was asked to do all the dirty jobs in the workshop area, such as sweeping floors, picking up rubbish, etc. During that time, Alan learnt to chase his wages because they were often overlooked; such was his status.

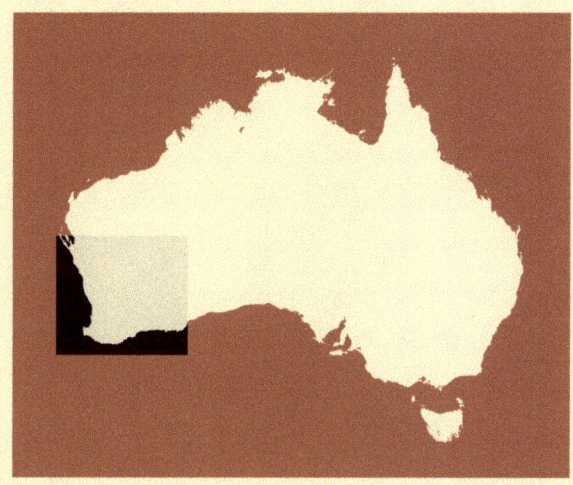

- Geraldton

- Kalgoorlie

## Wheatbelt

Fremantle • • PERTH • Bruce Rock
Mandurah • Corrigin • • Kondinin
Narrogin • • Wickepin
Bunbury • • Collie

## South West

## Great Southern District

• Albany

Alan Parsons during his Christ Church Grammar School days c.1944

## CHAPTER FOUR

# *"All up, I went to eleven schools"*
## *Alan Parsons*

### *The getting of wisdom*

Alan's first position with the International Harvester Company as 'shit-boy', terminated when he was thirteen. His grandmother Ede Parsons sold up in 1942, and went to live in a house in Seventh Avenue, Inglewood, Perth. Alan was again sent to live with her, this time to keep his grandmother company during some of the difficult war years. It also served to keep Alan in school. Brian, his little brother, remained with their parents on their farm and continued to attend Kunjin school.

Unbeknownst to Alan at the time, this location was unusually close to the relatives of his future wife, Mavis. Her Aunty Ethel, Uncle Sydney and her beloved cousin June, lived in Sixth Avenue, the very next street. It is even possible Alan went to the same school as June or that a young Mavis and Alan even passed each other in the street.

During the early part of city life in Inglewood, Alan fell off his bike, no doubt because of shenanigans, incurring yet another nasty wound that slowed him down for a time. His grandmother was ill-equipped to tend to the dreadful wound to his shin

*June Mansell at home
Sixth Avenue, Inglewood in 1942*

and the complications of living in a big city made it difficult to seek medical attention, so it lingered in a festering manner for months.

Nevertheless, Inglewood was where Alan felt his happiest. He was becoming older and could take on more responsibility. He could chop wood and fix anything that needed repairing. Being able to exercise his decision-making skills regarding the care of his grandmother, her daughter Ivy, and her house, made Alan feel worthy. He even found a good friend, a red-headed boy called Hawkins, who lived on the other side of the road. They went to the same school and both felt the kindred benefit of friendship.

During this friendship an event occurred which rocketed Alan to a new position at the school. Whilst at Inglewood Primary School he broke a record for 'the cuts'. At that school, teachers were not supposed to hand out more than six cuts a day. However, when Alan dared to 'back chat' the grimly-dressed teacher, this was not the case. The teacher's behaviour was questionable (he was prone to patting the girls a little too affectionately and had a spiteful attitude towards the boys), and provoked Alan into rebellion. The teacher, who wore the same black suit every day, planted twelve cuts on Alan's hand with a three-foot cane, six in the morning and then another six in the afternoon. Alan became the playground hero for the short-duration he attended that school.

Whilst working like a Trojan at her household chores, Ede still cared for her eldest daughter, Ivy, who lived her uncomplicated, silent life. Once Ede passed away, Ivy went to live in a home, but while she remained under Ede's wing, Ivy was always accepted as she was. It seems Ede was never far from the teapot because everyone would call in for a nice cup of tea; Ede's ability to provide love, caring and warmth, made all her homes the nucleus for family and friends.

Ede lived on until 1958, but Alan did not stay with her. His father, Cliff, sent him to support his Aunt Ella, who lived on her own while her husband, Wilf, was in the army (although it was unclear whether he went to war). Aunt Ella had been a nurse and lived in a house in Greenmount overlooking Perth. Alan rode down Greenmount Hill every day to attend Greenmount High School. He then rode all the way back up the hill to get home. Alan thinks he was sent to Aunt Ella to keep her company.

*Ede Parsons with her brother Walter Bland. Ivy is in the background with her doll, Perth 1940s*

In Greenmount, Alan made friends with a family of about twelve or thirteen children who lived up the road from Aunt Ella. They were very poor but very generous and Alan would sometimes go to play there and was invited to join them for meals and even stayed over once.

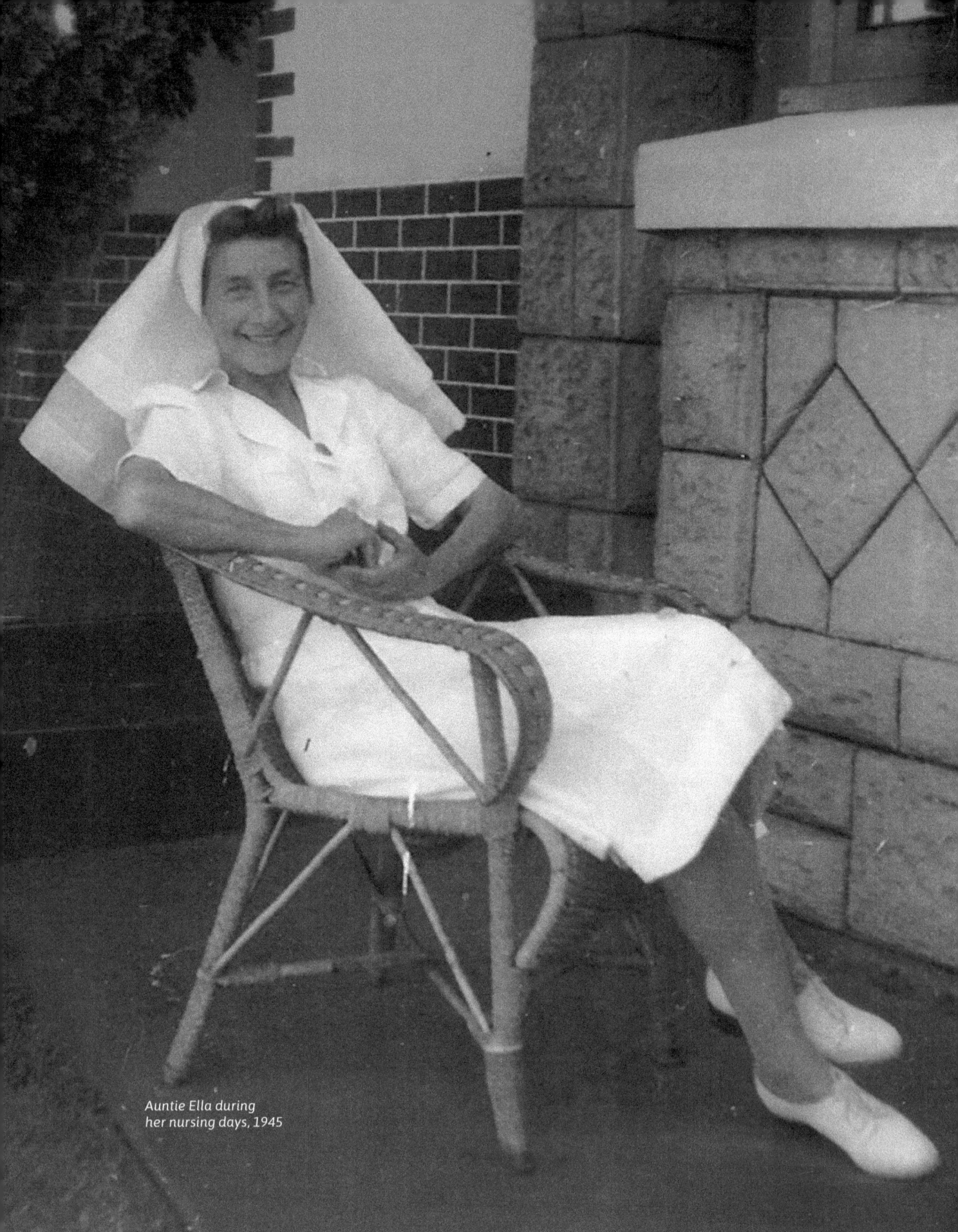

*Auntie Ella during her nursing days, 1945*

## *Back to the bush*

In 1943, Alan returned to live with his family on the farm they were leasing in Kunjin. Not long after, Cliff bought a farm east of Corrigin and the family ceased leasing and went to live on their newly-owned farm. A thousand acres for three thousand pounds: a bargain! Farming appeared to be quite profitable at that time with the harvest bringing in good money. This meant Cliff was soon able to purchase a second neighbouring farm of 1,200 acres for £1,200. By adding the adjoining farm, he increased his acreage to 2,200 acres. He paid for the lot within an astonishing two years.

*Cliff and Alma Parsons Corrigin farmhouse, mid 1940s*

However, the real reason this platter of opportunity had arrived was because of the dreadful hardship experienced by many vulnerable and inexperienced farmers. The government had veiled the misfortune experienced by those who had no choice but to leave their homes and dreams behind. These people had faced enormous challenges and, as Andrea Gaynor writes in her essay, *How to Eat a Wilderness*, their decisions to leave rode on the back of not only inexperience but also other variables like 'prices that fell and rain that failed, to salt and locusts and boredom ... for many new farmers, crop failure one year meant lack of money to buy seed wheat for the next.'

*The Argus* (a Melbourne, Victoria, newspaper) reported severe weather conditions in WA on Wednesday the 4th of December 1940:

> *W.A. DROUGHT BROKEN: HAIL RUINS CROPS. After probably the worst drought in the State's history, heavy rain fell throughout the farming areas yesterday and throughout last night. It was accompanied in places by disastrous hail and wind. Areas which had suffered drought most, received between one and two Inches of rain; the heaviest fall reported was 463 points [100 points to an inch] at Corrigin.*

For some, these hailstones were catastrophic; flattening crops ripe for the harvest as well as damaging farm buildings, windmills, trucks, farm machinery and cars. In some places in WA, the hail was over a foot (30 centimetres) deep.

After the drought broke, farmers had the luck of good harvests. Life appeared to be prosperous for the Parsons family and halfway through Alan's fourteenth year (1943) he was suddenly sent to Christ Church Grammar for almost eighteen months. Alan and his speech impediment were to be further challenged.

## *Christ Church Grammar School*

At Christ Church Grammar School, a private boys' school in Claremont, Perth, Alan was a boarder. It cost £100 per term, which led to Alan being threatened by his father; he had to learn or else!

He could ride his bike to visit his Great Aunt and Uncle Shannon, his mother's foster parents, who lived at 54 Minora Road, Dalkeith. Already savvy, young Alan asked a household whose property was near the school, if he could store his bike at their house when he wasn't using it. They agreed.

Despite Cliff's threat to 'do well or else', Alan's education took a backward step at this school. WWII took the young teachers off to fight for their country, with the result that the school brought in some old and decrepit, retired teachers who had long since had their day. It was easy for a young boy to fall off the rails; getting up to mischief was far more interesting than any lessons these elderly gentlemen tutors offered and Alan was right there in the thick of the nonsense.

One boarding school story took place at the boarding house called Queenslea, which was once a gracious two-storey home overlooking the Swan River. Donny Fulwood, Mick Moore and Alan Parsons were allocated a three-bedded room on the big wide verandah that circled the home. This was considered special by the boys because all the other dormitories had a prefect presiding to control behaviour.

This room had a wooden balustrade and a canvas blind on one side, which was lovely in the summer but freezing in winter. It also had a trapdoor going down into a cellar, which, of course, the curious young boys could not wait to check out. Although they could not see any benefits in the dark and damp cellar, some of the prefects knew it was there and made good use of it, smoking their cigarettes down there after lunch.

The following story is typical of Alan's time at Christ Church Grammar School. One day, Alan had a bright idea that his room-mates should help him do something about these arrogant prefects who barged into their dorm every day. The next time the prefects snuck down into the cellar to puff away on their smokes, the young boys carried a huge limestone rock up from the garden and placed it on the trapdoor, plus a couple of beds as extra weight, then they innocently went back to class knowing the prefects could not report them as they should not have been there in the first place. The prefects eventually got out around 3pm and, predictably, wrecked the boys room, throwing things everywhere.

Regardless of the havoc, the boys enjoyed a good laugh but had to quickly remove the evidence. Alan had another bright idea and coerced Donny into lifting the limestone block onto the balustrade and letting it fall about twelve feet into the garden below where the plan was that Alan would roll it back to where he found it. What they did not know was that there was an underground water-main right where the rock would land. Consequently, upon impact, the pipe immediately burst, sending forth a waterspout about six metres into the air. Alan moved quickly to remove the block and naturally got completely soaked in the process.

While the new 'water feature' attracted considerable attention, as the teachers arrived, followed by the matron, the headmaster, and finally the plumbers, no-one knew it was anything to do with those three boys except, of course, the prefects who were now sworn to secrecy for fear of their own exposure. To this very day, the mysterious water fountain has remained an unexplained phenomenon.

Well before the end of 1944, disgraced with dreadful grades, fifteen-year-old Alan was removed from the prestigious school and returned home to work on his parent's new farm. His father was convinced Alan would never amount to anything. Overall, because of WWII, the Depression and a lack of school buses, Alan attended eleven schools, giving him a somewhat incomplete and fragmented education.

Alan says it was farming that taught him his life skills. He learnt how to work with the discipline required to succeed. His background became the reason for his future success in business in the southwest of WA.

## Alan's full-time working life begins

Once on the job on his father's proudly-owned new farm, it was apparent it needed a great deal of work. Alan humbly and diligently applied himself; so much so that, after a few short weeks, his parents suddenly decided they could up and take a full six-week holiday, leaving fifteen-year-old Alan to run the property.

Apparently, his father could not afford to pay Alan wages but, after 1946, he did eventually lend Alan his truck so that the industrious young man could participate in share farming and oat carting, to earn himself a living while he lived on the Kunjin farm. Alan had been carting and driving different loads around the farm since he was twelve-years-old. However, as it took two to load a truck, with one on the ground lifting the bags up to the tray and the other on the tray stacking them, Alan found himself learning to expertly stack on the tray. This he did very well, with no loss of any part of any load in all the years he carted. He didn't drive on the roads until after he had arrived home from Christ Church in late 1946 at the age of fifteen. Alan says:

*I was always on the tray so I could stack the bags properly. I never lost a load, unlike a lot of farmers or carriers. I used to employ the local police officers when they had days off because of their weekend rosters. They were in shock when I turned 17 and went in to apply for my driver's license. For several years I had a full license, from motor bikes to the biggest trucks and semi-trailers, complements of these guys who enjoyed earning a few extra dollars.*

*Truck loaded with bags of oats Corrigin c.1948*

In the latter half of the 1940s, Alan and his Uncle Keith (Muir) worked together for several years carting wheat at harvest time. Keith had a truck with a tip body, whilst Alan's father's truck was a tray top. They travelled and worked in tandem, helping each other to load and unload. Before Keith's return journey back to Mandurah, he would call into the Corrigin tip and collect a backload of more refundable and recyclable goods. Keith made some good contacts and often carted superphosphate to Corrigin, making the round trip quite profitable.

*Brian Parsons during his student days at Narrogin Agricultural College c.1949*

## *Alan's brother Brian*

Alan's brother, Brian Parsons, did not attend anywhere near the same number of schools as Alan. Being five years younger had made Brian's life that much more secure, with the populations of rural WA increasing enough to enable him to stay with his parents whilst attending nearby schools. Brian could work on the farm and absorb the farming practices developed by his Corrigin farming relatives. In his early- to mid-teens, he attended Narrogin Agricultural College.

Brian grew up to enjoy a privileged social life in the, now well-established, Corrigin district. Luxurious facilities, like tennis courts, a bowling green and golf links, along with a magnificent town hall and hotel, and one of the best showgrounds in rural WA, made for a strong community. Many of the sporting facilities were made possible through the selfless work of his grandfather, George Parsons.

*Corrigin Hotel still with verandahs; not far up the street was the hostel Ede ran c.1940s*

On 8th November 1937, *The West Australian* newspaper published an article titled *History Of Corrigin: Wheat and Wool Production*. The article describes how beautifully the small town had developed since 1908, saying that in just 30 years the town went from a siding on the rail line between Perth and Southern Cross, to an excellent example of early pioneering spirit and industriousness.

Not only did Grandfather George Parsons contribute to Corrigin but he also worked tirelessly during their time in Narrogin 1908-32. Both towns commemorated George for his efforts in public undertakings, in his obituary in The Corrigin Chronicle, 9th May 1940 (see Appendix III).

In 1914, the rail link between Wickepin and Corrigin was completed. According to the State's Heritage council, by 1929 one of Western Australia's largest and most ornate town halls was built. It was said to be the finest structure of its kind outside of Perth, reflecting optimism and expansion as hundreds of returned soldiers took up land under the Soldier Settlement Scheme.

The town earned a reputation for its abundant fanfare of windmills accessing the generous supply of groundwater. The article went on to describe the setting for continuing social opportunities in a rich, close-knit community:

> *The town of Corrigin is situated close to the railway station, the outskirts being on rising ground. A fine hall, built at a cost of £8,000, stands almost at the corner of the two main streets. Corrigin also possesses a big State hotel and fine hospital and commercial buildings. A bowling green, tennis courts and golf links have been laid out, and the town possesses one of the best-situated showgrounds in the State. The streets are planted with hundreds of trees, but the town lacks one essential [facility]—an adequate water scheme. There is no lack of well water, but this is so impregnated with magnesia that when it is used frequently on gardens, the soil becomes infertile. Used on lawns and grasses, the water has no ill effect.*

Even though lawn bowls now is often considered a pastime for older folk, in Corrigin during the 1940s and 50s it was enjoyed by all ages due to the accessibility of the sport. Alan Parsons certainly maintained proud ownership of a set of original 1950s lawn bowling balls all his adult life, although, once living in Bunbury, no-one ever saw him use them.

Brian was attending Narrogin Agriculture College when Alan bought his first car, a 1926 Buick sedan with a canvas hood. The previous owner, farmer Jack Trott, had put a gas producer on it during the war years. Alan acquired it just after the war, when the government implemented fixed prices. At the time, there were very few cars around. Alan paid £57 10s. He then converted it to a farm ute; Alan says he converted it just because he could. It seems his Muir uncle's influence prevailed.

*Alan's first car, a Buick sedan, which he converted into a ute in 1946*

*Brian and Alan with their mother Alma Parsons alongside Alan's bench seat Chevy, which also had a Dickie seat in the back discovered by opening the boot, 1951*

Brian developed a close association with his neighbours, the Haydons, although it could be argued Brian's association favoured Mary, their youngest daughter. Mary was a devout homebody from the start, especially proven when she was sent to board at Northam High School so that she could complete her schooling. She only lasted a few days before she arrived back home, declaring she would not return. Her people were German in origin and possessed strong family roots, heralding from South Australia. Jack, her father, worked at an agricultural college before he, his wife and children came to WA in the 1930s. Mary and Brian (aged 20) were married in 1954 at Wesley Church, Perth, and subsequently lived on Brian's parents farm for three years before moving to Mary's parent's property to pursue their farming livelihood. Mary had a great understanding of growing produce and all aspects associated with a farming property. In that way, the young couple made a strong and committed partnership as part of Corrigin's mainstay farmers.

During farming's tough times, Brian drove a truck for some seven years. Together Mary and Brian raised their four children, Rhonda, Leeanne, Steven and Tracey, followed by nine grandchildren and seventeen great grandchildren. Steven Parsons is

*Brian (7/6/1934 - 8/8/2023) and Mary Parsons (née Haydon 1/1/1933 - 7/5/2022) on their wedding day (17/7/1954). Alma (Brian and Alan's mother) is in the background*

the only male of the eight children between Alan and Brian to carry on the Parsons' name, from Cliff Parsons' lineage. Steven forged a career working at the Shell Depot in Corrigin before he discovered his real passion, driving trucks, notably fuel tankers, all over the country. Brian too drove trucks all his working life, and like the Muirs, delved into the scrap metal industry, although more as a money raising venture for his many community projects.

Both Brian and Mary were involved with various organisations in the town, but were widely recognised (as was Cliff before them) for their contribution to the Corrigin Agricultural Society. In 1986 Brian was the president of 'The Eastern Districts Show Group', with Mary as secretary; both worked hard to inspire and manifest the presentation of one of the best displays ever on record at the Royal Show (winning fourteen awards). Brian went on to become president of the Agricultural Society in the early 1990s and both Mary and Brian were presented with life memberships of the society.

Alan may not have gone on to play bowls, but Mary sure did, eventually becoming a fully qualified umpire. But it didn't stop there, Mary's sporting prowess stretched across to tennis and hockey where she became one of the best hockey players in the district.

In later years, Brian contributed greatly to the Corrigin Pioneer Museum. He was both vice president and president of it covering some twenty years. All up Brian worked tirelessly preserving history for forty-three years. Mary was the museum's curator for twenty-one years, during which time she kept a beautifully hand scrolled ledger of all the museum's contents. Brian and others have maintained the upkeep of old tools, restored farm machinery and a blacksmith shop as well as numerous other pioneer memorabilia. The following is taken from the Corrigin website:

> *CORRIGIN PIONEER MUSEUM. Housing the history of our days gone by, a worthwhile visit whilst in Corrigin. View the collection of tools and restored farm machinery, including tractors in working order, see the blacksmith's shop, the one room school, the shearing shed, old district photographs, clothing and other pioneer memorabilia. The Pioneer Memorial Wall at the entrance to the Museum commemorates early settlers.*

In the 1950s, with both her sons married and raising their own families, Alma found herself called upon to nurse her foster mother, Alice Shannon. This happened after Jack Shannon had died, so Alma went to live in the Shannon's home in Dalkeith, Perth. When Alice passed away she left Alma the house. This was the first time Alma had ever had anything of her own.

When Cliff was 49, he left the farm he and Alma owned in Brian's hands, then aged 20, who thereupon managed the property. During this period Brian and Mary built on a three bedroom home for their growing family. Cliff moved into the house at 54 Minora Road with Alma, taking a job with an insurance company as a Hail Assessor for the Wheatbelt. This meant he travelled rural WA during the spring/summer months, often working away for lengthy periods. Strangely, a short time later, Cliff, without notice to Brian or the family, sold the farm leaving everyone flummoxed. He then began a series of untimely property investments, until he found himself in financial difficulty in the 1960s.

*Alma Parsons inherits the Shannon's home at 54 Minora Road Dalkeith.
This was a game changer for Alma c.1954*

*Alice and Jack Shannon c.1950.
This childless couple raised Alma Muir as their own*

*From left, Jack Haydon (Brian's father-in-law), Cliff Parsons, and Paddy Wright (who started the Corrigin Dog Cemetery) with a load of wool bales.*
*Photo taken towards the end of Cliff's Corrigin farming days c.1953*

CHAPTER FIVE

# *"I walked up and down the main street planning ways to check out the new girl in town"*
## *Alan Parsons*

### *Alan meets Mavis*

Mavis Horner moved to Corrigin with her parents in 1946 and soon secured a job in 'parts' at Spanney's, a farm machinery and spare parts Ford dealership. Alf Spanney was the Ford dealer, selling cars, trucks and tractors. He also ran the electrical power system for the town. Mavis was employed to run the parts department but very soon, became the secretary and office manager, doing a range of jobs: from ordering parts, recording all sales, doing wages (Mavis had authority to both write and sign cheques for the wages and all other payments), and the banking. She was required to check the petrol bowsers and was generally the second-in-charge to Alf, who also had a couple of farms and was often not on the premises.

Alf Spanney had two daughters, Lorna and Betty, who were prone to ask Mavis to do little jobs for them. (Betty later reappeared in Mavis's life in Bunbury.) If that wasn't enough, Mrs Spanney, who was the secretary of the hospital committee, expected Mavis to help her with fund raising efforts when required.

*Alan Parsons setting off to drove the sheep into town c.1947*

*Mavis Horner headed to work at Spanney's in Corrigin c.1947*

Because Mavis worked behind the counter, she had direct contact with customers. The day came when Alan finally went in to buy, of all things, torch batteries and Mavis served him. Alan says of the experience: 'I was instantly lit up!'

The exchange must have indeed been electric as Mavis remembers a special moment not long after their initial contact, when she was walking to work one morning. There was not a soul on the street except a lone rider on horseback in the distance. His stirrups were long, his slouch hat heavy over his eyes. As they slowly moved towards one another, Mavis was taking it all in when she suddenly realised she was looking at Alan, and her heart gave a little start. He had just finished droving a mob of sheep into town. They scarcely spoke as they passed one another, but by then, Mavis was smitten and utterly captivated by this young man.

Unfortunately, due to Alan's friend Donny Fulwood, and his efforts in shoring up Alan, Mavis did not know which one was courting her for some time. It was not until one of Corrigin's country balls, held in the town hall, that it became clear. Clarity came from an unexpected source: Mavis, who was accepting one dance after another from potential suitors, recalls encountering Alma, Alan's mother.

Alma, who was very involved with the community, sitting on several committees as well as actively catering for events, had sized up the situation. Alan was away that evening, believed to be keeping an appointment in Perth with a speech therapist to overcome his childhood stutter. As was her practise, Alma was working hard providing the supper, when she noticed Mavis was always on the dance floor. Alma knew Alan was fond of Mavis, so in her subtle way she sidled up to Mavis at the supper table and delicately reprimanded her. Mavis then knew and understood Alan's intent.

However, as Alan could not attend the ball that evening, he had appointed his mate, Donny to be guardian of Mavis. Mavis wasn't told of this agreement and so the situation became confused after Alma's little chat. At the end of the ball, Donny tried to walk Mavis home, but when he went into the hall to retrieve his jacket, Mavis lifted her skirts and made a run for it. She was home before he even made it back to the hall doorway.

## *Mavis's family*

Mavis was first generation Australian; she and her cousin June were the only ones in the family group of eleven to be born in Australia. Mavis was brought up in a house full of adults. Her sister, Nancy (or Phyllis), was some eleven years older and made sure Mavis did everything she told her to do.

The age difference occurred because Nancy was a half-sister, with different fathers. Nancy's father was an educated man, a chemist from London, while Mavis's father was an illiterate farm hand from Edinburgh. Mavis's parents, having arrived separately from the UK, soon found themselves living in the Corrigin district in the early 1920s. At that stage Annie, her mother, was still married to Clement Wood with a five-year-old daughter. The little family had taken up land at Kondinin and were attempting to fulfil their commitment to the government to clear it, when a dreadful accident occurred in 1924, which changed everything.

*Sisters Ethel and Annie with Annie's daughter Nancy and the sisters' mother, Ann Hall*

The first of the family group to leave England were Mavis's grandparents, James Walter Hall, and his wife Ann Hall (née Moult) arrived in Fremantle in December 1919, on board the Orsova. It is not apparent where they went or what they did until their daughters and their husbands arrived the following year. This second group embarked in London on the Borda on the 3rd of June 1920, and consisted of Annie Wood, her husband Clement Wood, and their five-year-old daughter Nancy Phyllis Wood; Ethel Mansell (née Hall) and her husband newspaper journalist Sydney Mansell; and another man, Walter Newton, also a journalist. It eventuated that this group was to share a Kondinin property through a government land grant registered to all three men. The former British soldiers each had a homestead lot of 160 acres.

*Annie and Clement Wood's wedding 30 October 1912*
Back row from left: Mr & Mrs Mansell, Alec Wood, Wally Hall, Mr Wood,
Ann & James Hall, Sydney Mansell, friend, Mr & Mrs Wood senior, Mr & Mrs Elesume.
Front row from right: Louie Hall, Clement & Annie Wood (née Hall), Ethel Hall

It is unclear how they travelled to Kondinin, but they may have taken the train from Perth to Narrogin because the railway line from Yilliminning to Kondinin started in 1913 and the Kondinin Loop Line from Yilliminning to Kondinin opened on 15th March 1915.

It is known that there were shacks on the property and that they shared a horse and cow between them. But they also shared the numerous snakes and goannas. Stories abound of the easily spooked racehorse goanna being prone to run up any close vertical object, be it human, horse, post or tree. The cow enabled them to survive on its milk and thereby produce cream and butter. What remains a puzzle is how these professional people, straight from Stockport, UK, would have had any idea about how to begin farming the land in Western Australia. Surely a very bad state of affairs was to come?

*ill v:* Graphite drawing of sisters Annie and Ethel at the Kondinin Co-op store in the 1920s, inspired by a historic photograph on display near the pioneer wall in Kondinin. The pioneer wall shows the names of Ethel and Sydney Mansell, Annie and Clement Wood, and Walter Newton and indicates the location of their farm.

The land around Kondinin opened up for selection in 1910. It was heavily timbered land with rich red soil.

In 1924, whilst trying to save the horse from a difficult situation loading water at the dam, Clement drowned. It is said the horse must have kicked him in the head. The story implies he was trying to unhitch the water cart, which had slid into the dam taking the horse with it.

After a year of correspondence back and forward to the U.K, in the endeavour to locate a will from his army days, a vital letter posted in England reached its destination in Kondinin with the extraordinarily vague address:

'MANSELL ESQUIRE, WESTERN AUSTRALIA'.

Even with the psychic powers of the Perth post office to pinpoint where in vast state of WA Mansell actually was, the news was not good. The Supreme Court ultimately declared that because Clement died without a will, the property could not be divided up. The property had to be sold quickly to clear the mounting debts. The family group moved to Perth. The property was sold the 6th of September 1926, to

C.E. Smithers, a notorious American opportunist in the Corrigin district. In a strange twist of fate, Mavis and Alan's families traded locations, passing each other in the night, so to speak. This very same Kondinin property then was managed by Cliff's brother Les Parsons and his wife Irene, who, with their daughter Audrey (who was eight at the time), lived on the farm for many years.

*Les and Irene Parsons with daughter Audrey around the time when Les managed the Kondinin property that Mavis's family had left in 1926*

Audrey, Alan's cousin, was eleven years older than Alan and remembers living there. Alan recalls his grandfather going to see Les and Irene, but as an adult Alan puzzled over its location for many years. Anne Elliott (née McGinnity), Ethel and Sydney Mansell's granddaughter, located it in 2015 through documents at the WA State Records Office. Alan, Mavis, Julie and Anne then went to Corrigin to unearth its position within the mammoth acreage of the property now owned by the Brownings. Discovering where the property was in relation to his grandfather's Emoh Ruo enabled Alan to see the previous family connection.

## *Mavis is born to Annie and William Horner*

Mavis Horner 1926

Once in Perth, Annie married William Horner, who had been helping the families clear the land at the time of Clement's accident. Bill (William) had stayed on to help Annie with her land grant commitment to clear the land. Over the three years it took to resolve the property issues their relationship changed and Annie fell pregnant with Mavis. The marriage in Perth was therefore a rushed affair. Annie felt great shame about this and tried to change the year of birth on Mavis's birth certificate.

Mavis was born in Perth on 19 June 1926. Bill managed to find work on the railways and Annie, with her two daughters and Bill, found a home at 10 Essex Street, Wembley, where they lived for around fourteen years.

When Bill was transferred to a job on the railways in Bunbury, Annie's first daughter Nancy had already left home. The family of three moved to Beach Road, Bunbury. At this stage, Mavis, in her early teens, did a bookkeeping course, which was followed with a job in the office at Bunbury Hospital, before Bill was again transferred. In another interesting twist to the family story they found themselves back in Corrigin. Mavis was about nineteen and had chosen to move with her parents.

Bill, a Scotsman, had never learnt to read or write, so, while they lived in Corrigin, Mavis's mother, Annie, helped and supported Bill to achieve literacy, which in turn enabled him to pursue job advancement. Her mother's role-modelling of this achievement showed Mavis what was possible with a little support.

*Mavis Horner with Alan Parsons' Chevy during their courtship c.1949*

Mavis and Alan Parsons' wedding 1951.
Mavis wore a rich ivory satin brocade gown which, along with her mother's wedding gown, is still in the family's possession (shown in photo 5:5)

## Wooing Mavis

After several social skirmishes and realignment to the correct courtship candidate, Mavis was on track to become Mrs Alan Parsons. Even though the planets were aligned in this matter, the reality was that Alan was not yet twenty-one, and was still considered a boy. He did not have enough behind him to set up for married life. Mavis was three years older and had been working on her glory box for some time. The contents of a glory box were usually homemaking items that a girl was given, collected or made. Relatives also contributed to this masterful concept. Most of the contents were handmade necessities like tea towels, face cloths or embroidered linen, perhaps a tea set or cutlery and the like. Generally, it was all about setting up a home. Each object was adored and filled with all the reverence and expectation a young woman was encouraged to hold.

In time, Alan bought an old Austin truck to continue his carting work. During the 1950 harvest he cleared £3,000 with the truck in one six-week season. He worked completely on his own during this season. The income he raised enabled him to consider marriage with a possibility of putting down the deposit for a farm.

Alan married Mavis on 10 January 1951, when he was just 21.

## The beginning of married life

According to Mavis, on their wedding day (a hot, windless day in January), the moment they were declared man and wife a mysterious wind took the curtains in the church and blew them high. This auspicious event took place at Christ Church on Stirling Highway, Claremont, opposite Alan's former boarding school.

For the first eight months, they lived in a homemade caravan, which they parked under a peppermint tree on Alan's parent's property, near the household facilities. Caravans in the first half of the twentieth century were often handmade and were very small, as was theirs. They could cook and sleep in it but not much else.

*Mavis Parsons outside the little caravan with farm dog, c.1951*

Mavis says of the eight months living in close quarters with her in-laws, that she felt she never got to first base with Alan's mother, Alma. She seemed to be protective about Alan and perhaps, because of his stutter, she worried Mavis might not stand by him. But Mavis was absolutely committed. She says she was determined to listen well to all that Alan said, always stopping what she was doing to do so. She stood directly in front of Alan, making eye contact and giving him the time he needed to find security in her presence. She listened well.

Alan's father Cliff was a complex man: he could be light-hearted one minute and heavy going the next. As Mavis's father, Bill, worked on the railways he often encountered Cliff Parsons, whom he described as an abrasive man. As mentioned, Bill could not read and write, so he was compromised. Whilst living in Corrigin with her parents, Mavis had observed her mother, Annie, patiently supporting Bill in his effort to conquer reading and writing. This action set the stage for Mavis to support Alan in overcoming his childhood stutter.

With Mavis's approval, Alan chose a property in Gorge Rock. Once they secured the purchase of their own property, they then lived in the uncomplicated farmhouse, which was a simple three-roomed building with a kitchen, lounge and bedroom. It was constructed with unpainted weatherboard. Alan bought some second-hand machinery and some sheep, and then got a tax bill for £500 (which of course, he did not have).

The pair slowly painted and added to their home, and before long, Mavis was pregnant with her first born. Mavis was a singer and the house and family car trips were always filled with song despite his stutter, Alan joined in with ease. Together, Alan and Mavis sometimes made the long and tedious trip to Perth to continue Alan's commitment with the speech therapist. Alan also made the trip alone for several more years.

Their farmhouse was fenced-in, allowing livestock to graze around the yard. Inside the fence they kept a pet lamb, which became a rambunctious wether. This pet patrolled the house fence-line allowing no-one easy access, but this made departures very tricky. Allan White, a courageous neighbour whose farm was on the other side of the gravel main road, would occasionally drive over to visit the household. He drove a little old Prefect car from the back seat, because the driver's seat had disintegrated so he simply removed it. His ability to repair was plainly impaired as he also drove a truck from which he had to enter and exit via the window due to a broken door. His skills with a shotgun were likewise dodgy when he attempted to shoot a black snake in the washhouse, instead blowing the entire wall out. Needless to say, upon entering the Parsons' house paddock, he often encountered the said lamb.

Not without incident, the interaction between the two developed into a comical affair. Allan White invented a technique of beating a big stick on the ground, chasing the lamb up the fence line, then turning and running like heck to his car to get in and drive through the gate before the lamb realised. The problem was the lamb frequently beat him back and the whole process had to be repeated. Mavis always watched this — falling about laughing till tears fell down her cheeks.

## *Peter the farm dog*

*Julie Parsons with the family farm dog called Peter who turned her away from the dam in the top paddock c.1956*

On one of Alan and Mavis's trips to Perth, they happened across a pet shop in London Court. In the window was a small terrier puppy which caught Mavis's eye. The unity was instant and so compelling that Alan was sent in to ask, 'How much is that doggy in the window?' He bought the pup for Mavis and they called him Peter, and thereafter had the best farm dog (although unlike any other) they could have ever wished for.

Even though it was Mavis who connected with Peter the pup, it also connected with Alan because Alan was where all the action was happening. Peter accompanied Alan on all his farm chores and along the way learned the language and commands for sheepdogs. Once he learnt that, he could work the sheep with the best of them, his greatest trick being to run along their backs to keep them moving. He always travelled in the front cab of the truck with Alan and even went to town on business, sitting there with all the prowess of second-in-charge. As a character and unlikely farm dog he became affectionately well-known and respected amongst Alan's mates.

Mavis and Alan became parents. First came a daughter they called Julie. Two years later another daughter they named Eleanor and two years later yet another daughter they named Susan. But more about that later. When Mavis was busy with baby Susan, and toddler Eleanor, four-year-old Julie would set off to entertain herself, frequently accompanied by the trusty Peter.

Julie's personal memories of Peter were that he must have been everywhere at once, because she believed he was her perpetually attentive playmate. Julie's fondest memory is when he accompanied her, aged 4, on a stroll picking dandelion flowers. Once she got motoring, and out of sight of the farmhouse, she was filled with the explorer's urge to see what was over the next hill. Julie reports Peter's behaviour changed when she was well over the hill and into the paddock with the dam. He began to round her up trying to divert her from her intention. Both determined beings, he went one way and she went the other. But it was no fun without him so Julie turned to see where he was. He was eyeballing her from the gate with all his body language pointing home. Naturally Julie went back to get him but he kept just that tiny bit in front of her with his new exciting game of 'catch me if you can' until they were safely back at the farm house. Clever dog that one.

## *The daily milking*

*Peter and Roanie the cow 1956*

Peter slept in a kennel outside the house. The rattle of the milk bucket first thing in the morning signalled the day's work had begun and he was up and ready for action. The immediate job of the day was to feed and milk Roanie, their shorthorn cow. Roanie occupied a ten-acre paddock next to the shearing shed and dined on hay and oats whilst the milking took place. Alan always took a wet cloth from the house to clean the udder and teats. Milking was a twice-a-day job. The milk was taken back to the house for straining. Next came separating the cream, churning it and patting it into butter. Alan describes their technique:

*We had a separator in the laundry. We would put the milk in the bowl on top and then we would turn the handle, which would revolve cups that would send the heavier cream to the outer rim then into a bowl. The separated milk would first be fed to the calf until it was weaned, then fed to the pigs to help fatten them. We would keep back milk required for ourselves before sharing it with the animals.*

*Mavis would make butter with wooden patties after beating and thickening some of the cream. We then had fresh milk, cream and butter. If we had excess, Mavis would sell butter in town or supply her parents who still lived in Corrigin. If the cow got cross and kicked the bucket, all was lost. That was a real hazard and you had to be alert to the possibility.*

All the above had to be done before breakfast and then out to do the day's work repeating the same at night no matter how exhausted.

At first, they managed to store the milk products in their Coolgardie Safe, which was a wooden frame covered with wire mesh. A hessian bag was draped over a galvanised iron tray on top. The tray was filled with water and the hessian bag was hung over the side with one of the ends in the water, soaking it up. Once the bag was completely wet and the breeze was passing through the hessian, the water would slowly evaporate, cooling the air and food inside the safe. A metal tray was usually placed to catch any dripping water at the bottom. The Coolgardie Safe lived in the vestibule just off the back verandah, to catch the breeze from the 'Albany Doctor'. These cooling safes were still being used all over Australia in the 1950s; however, the thrill of a kerosene fridge was soon upon them.

## *The mod cons*

Alan says: 'The first fridge we had was a kerosene version, that burnt a flame 24/7. The flame activated the refrigerant and kept all inside cold. We could even make ice cream'. For the first four years on the property, the young family used kerosene lamps as their light source in the evenings and at pre-dawn, just as many settlers had done before them. Once the new 32-volt generator was purchased and set up in the garage, it supplied a bank of batteries that stored the power. The motor drove a generator that generated power to charge the batteries. Lights etc. were not to be left on as power would be wasted. The engine had to be running if the 32-volt iron was being used, as it would flatten the batteries quickly. Mavis could only iron if Alan was around to start the engine.

The same applied for the telephone. To achieve a phone line required Alan to erect poles and wire from the Downing's farm, about four or five kilometres away, but because the technology of the day only supplied a party line, they would not have been able to use the phone if the Downings were not at home. Alan declined the opportunity.

## *Water and the Gorge Rock farmhouse*

The farmhouse was about a kilometre from the main gravel road, on a small rise with a hill behind it. Upon seeing anyone driving through the front gate, Mavis had just the right amount of time to make a batch of scones. Provided the stove was lit and the urn of water was boiling, visitors would be served these freshly baked scones with a nice cup of tea.

The hot water for the farmhouse was kept in the stove-top urn, with a tap, and placed on the side of the stove's wood box above the oven. This provided hot water for washing up, making pots of tea, and baths. A copper for washing clothes was in the laundry, an outhouse, where it was set into a brick and cement structure with a firebox underneath and a chimney to carry the smoke outside. The water was put into the copper and was heated by lighting a fire in the firebox. To do this the copper was filled, with buckets, from the distant rainwater tank. A dipper and a pair of large wooden tongs were used to get the clothes in and out of the boiling hot water. Understanding the sheer muscle power required to lift the scorching hot articles from the boiling water without getting scalded needs to be appreciated. The heavy bed linen and towels were the worst, along with the daily, danger-filled grind of extracting scalding hot, cotton nappies from the boiling water with a mere 'copper stick', in order to keep a supply of hygienically cleaned, fresh nappies for the babies.

Rainwater tanks supplied the household with water when available but water had to be carted to the parched property during the long, hot, and dry summer months. The water came from a bore sunk 100 metres from Gorge Rock Pool, a rain catchment area. Alan would load two, empty, 400-gallon metal tanks onto the back of his truck and head to the water bore, a five-kilometre trip. The bore supplied overhead tanks filled by the action of a windmill pumping water from the bore into the tanks. A pipe came out of the overhead tanks, which had a big tap on it. By driving the truck under the pipe Alan and the other farmers would turn the tap on and fill his tanks. No wind, no water. The heavy metal tanks then had to be unloaded to keep the truck available for other farm work.

*Gorge Rock farm house. Photo taken from the shed. A garage was built where the caravan stands c.1952*

Given the level of difficulty in obtaining it, water was extremely precious. Bath time was once a week and all the family had to bathe in the same tub of water - kids first, then Mavis, then Alan. Peeing in the bath was a criminal offense!

# The Gorge Rock swimming hole

Located 20 kilometres from Corrigin and five kilometres from the farm, Gorge Rock is a natural rock pool, which became the local swimming hole for the family. In the mid-1950s some of the local farmers had built a brick and stone wall around two big natural rock formations, creating a dam of water to become a summer swimming hole.

*Gorge Rock swimming hole (photo courtesy Corrigin Shire social history database) c.1956*

Alan and a nucleus of three to five farmers masterminded the idea and organised a number of 'working bees', which brought in another five or so farmers to help with the hard labour. Donations provided money for the cost of the netting and cement. Alan was the youngest farmer who worked on the concept and then its realisation. Some of the others were Max Lange, George Downing, Ted and Allan White, and Otto Prizabella (Prizzie).

According to Ross Haig, in his book *Corrigin*, commissioned by the Shire in 1982, the dam was fourteen feet deep at the wall and 225 feet long by 70 feet wide. The simple diving board as seen in the above picture (5:14), really set the scene. Interestingly, the pool's builders laid a five inch bore casing at the bottom, which enabled drainage at the end of each summer. The water was frequently sanitised to keep it safe for swimming during the hot summers.

Alan says a custom-built, ground level, shallow cement trough was a made to which Condi's crystals were added to the ankle high water. Before entering the Gorge Rock pool, swimmers had to walk through the shallow trough of purple water. This was thought to kill any unwanted nasties carried in on the feet.

Families were able to enjoy decades of cooling off, with picnics and social events at and around the pool. A family visit to the Gorge Rock hall for a Christmas celebration and dance or the like was not uncommon in the early days. Meetings too were often held at the hall, particularly when they were building the pool.

## *Goldsbrough Mort*

Alan's preferred Stock agency was Goldsbrough Mort (eventually bought out by Elders) and when Bill Matthews, the new young stock agent, came to town the two men, finding themselves at similar stages in their lives, formed a supportive bond.

*Goldsbrough Mort sale yards in Corrigin c.1957 (photo courtesy of Bill Matthews)*

Bill and Yvonne arrived in Corrigin in 1957, with babies underfoot. As was the way, Bill's young wife Yvonne and Mavis contented themselves with brief encounters when it suited the men folk. That is until they were able to join the local Repertory Club, where, according to Yvonne, "a 'point of unencumbered contact' was achieved for Mavis and I — particularly in musical productions — both performers by nature methinks."

They were young parents at the same time, but most of all the men were both strivers and wanted to be at the top of their game. Fortunately, both men possessed wives able to see the funny side of life, and both held a remarkable optimism for their futures regardless of life's little setbacks.

Bill helped Alan sort out what sheep to buy and sell, and how and where to buy and sell pigs. Bill's boss Stan Magee developed a healthy respect for Bill when he sent him out to a farm to buy some sheep. Bill went on to sell the sheep to another farmer, then suggested to that same farmer that it would be profitable to send them to Midland, where butchers would buy them. He earned three lots of commission for Goldsbrough that day, without touching the sheep.

Another such coup occurred while unloading a mob of sheep delivered by rail. According to Yvonne and Bill this is how the story went:

*Stan Magee had bought good sheep at a very acceptable price from a Bruce Rock farmer on spec. And rather than "turn them over" locally, he railed them to Matthews in Corrigin to "turn them over" — all grist to the Goldsbrough mill. As Bill was unloading in the railway yards a local farmer came sniffing about. Bill offered the same sheep to him at a further inflated price thus more profit for the firm. The deal duly done, Magee rang to enquire their fate only to be told, proudly, of the inflated sold-on price. He savagely chewed the young dog's ear, but later Matthews learned the boss bragged about his well taught, up and coming stock salesman.*

Thereafter, the two referred to one another in their own terms of reverence. Bill referred to his boss as 'Mr Magee', while Stan called his young colt, 'Matthews'.

*Alan Parsons loaded up with his farm clearing equipment*

## *The bloody hard work*

Gorge Rock farm was covered in Mallee roots and small rocks, which had to be cleared. Over five years, Alan carted 108 truckloads of Mallee roots to the Corrigin butcher for burning at the butcher's abattoir business.

Alan put in nine years of hard and difficult work on this farm. He suffered sunstroke three times. On the first occasion, Mavis, with very little driving experience or skill, had to drive to a neighbouring farm to call the doctor for advice. As the telephones functioned on a party line, which of course enabled others to listen in. From this call, Mavis learnt she had to help him into a cold-water bath in an attempt to bring his body heat back to normal.

One evening, after hours of seeding day and night during the winter months, Alan passed out at the table from sheer overwork. Flummoxed, Mavis thought he had died.

## *The pigs and the railway sleepers*

Alan kept 30 to 40 pigs, which he bred, then carted the occasional truckload to either Bruce Rock or Midland to sell at auction. He built his pigsty from old railway sleepers he'd bought for £1 per hundred and then slowly collected from beside the railway tracks. Mavis's father, a railway man, helped Alan by telling him the various locations where the sleepers were replaced and discarded alongside the railway lines. Foreseeing their value Alan collected some 500 sleepers.

With help from the local Stock agent Bill Matthews, who advised on markets and predicted variations of where best to buy and sell, Alan began to take his pigs to market. Matthews was young and new into the job and as mentioned, at about the same stage in life as Alan, allowing the two to became good mates. At the pig sales Alan would buy weaners to bring home and fatten up. Sometimes he would back load diesel or extra fuel for the farm machinery.

The pig sty area was a mass of mud and sludge in winter with a trough for water and a trough for the pig slops to be dropped into. Water was imperative in that area and was supplied by a rainwater tank attached to the shed. It had to be bucketed over to the pigs and the cow. If it ran dry Alan brought in water from the bore at Gorge Rock.

## The humpy and the help

During seeding time, Alan not only had to do the day-to-day farm work of feeding and watering the pigs, milking the cow, moving the sheep, checking the fences and stock, but also the seeding, which often meant working day and night. The job last thing at night was to load the truck with seed and 'super' for the next day. Alan would try to get a little sleep before starting seeding again at three in the morning. The first part of the procedure was to lay the super and the seed. This required the laborious action of driving the tractor either up and down, or in a spiralling circle, across the paddocks.

There was a humpy on the property, built from sawn timber, a few boards and covered in sheets of lumpy, old corrugated iron around an earthen floor. There were a couple of old iron beds and bedside tables made from small, old tin drums. There was an open fireplace to light a fire to keep warm or boil a kettle. Of course, there was no bathroom so occupants had to make their own arrangements in regard to washing and toileting. Mavis provided cooked meals. The humpy was designated for farm workers, usually one bloke at a time. Workmen would stay when they came to work during the busy times. One old retired fellow from Corrigin called Rod Stewart lived in the humpy for a year or so. He had an alcohol problem but worked hard when he could.

On another occasion Alan hired a young boy through a labour agency in Perth during the busy seeding time. The boy hated goannas with a vengeance and when he saw one would spend time digging a hole to bury it in. Unbeknown to the boy the goannas invariably dug themselves out. The boy claimed he was a former abattoir worker and volunteered to kill the sheep. Alan, always keen to learn a thing or two was up for the demonstration. Alan usually broke their neck and cut the throat with a knife in quick succession. The kid reckoned he knew how to do it better than that and began to show his knowhow.

He took the sheep and laid it across his legs and promptly cut not only its throat but sliced an impressive long, deep cut into his own leg as well. With blood and squeals everywhere Alan dropped the sheep and got the kid to hospital. He took the family's little Prefect car and drove him into town to be stitched up. In the meantime, the sheep had died and started to go off, so it could not be used for the family's fresh meat supply. Upon his return Alan buried it and got another sheep to do the whole thing all over again. Perhaps this should have been warning enough, but Alan wanted to give the boy a go.

One Friday afternoon, when Alan took the family to town for supplies, as was their practise, they had an appointment to attend in the evening. Alan set the boy up to plough a paddock in spiralling circles around a large stack of Mallee roots in the centre. There was nothing else in the paddock which might obstruct the action, so the instruction was simple. The stack was the size of a small dwelling. The job should have taken most of the night and when Alan returned expecting to take over he was immediately disturbed because he couldn't hear the tractor. There was no light from tractor headlamps in the paddock either ... all was still and dark.

Alan knew the boy should still be ploughing, but this kid was nowhere to be seen. Alan finally found him sound asleep in the humpy. When asked what he was doing, the boy explained that he could not do anymore because he didn't see the Mallee root stack and that the tractor and plough were stuck on it. He apparently drove the tractor and plough onto the top of the huge pile of Mallee roots. Furious, Alan stayed up most of the night trying to get his valuable machinery off the stack and ready for work the next day. Once he had done that he then loaded up the truck with all the super and seed needed for the next day.

The following morning, Alan sacked the boy and drove him into town leaving him at the station to catch the next train back to Perth, but apparently that didn't happen. The boy had walked over the road to the Council depot and asked for a job. The

Council workers were in for a surprise and the boy didn't disappoint.

While out doing some major roadworks using heavy tractors, the boy punctured one of the big tyres. As replacing the inner tube was no mean feat this was frowned upon. Once the replacement tube had been sourced the difficult job began., it required a number of men and some lengths of 4x2 to pry the heavy outer tyre away from the hub in order to pull the punctured inner tube out and replace it. Work could be held up for days while all this went on.

On this occasion, that was not the only problem. The men and the boy finally got the new tube in and pumped up ready to go. With the job completed the boy started the big tractor and began heading off up the road when all hell broke loose. Unbeknown to the workmen, 'someone' had left their length of 4x2 timber in the tyre casing. It went unnoticed because it was easy to pump up the inner tube, which swelled around it, but when the tractor wheel began to turn the timber pushed through the outer tyre and then splintered bursting the new inner tube. With the hub and both the tyre and the tube now damaged, work was stopped completely.

## *Nine years*

In those nine years, Mavis bore three daughters: Julie on 8th May 1953, Eleanor, 8th April 1955, and Susan, 8th March 1957. The odds of all three daughters being born on the 8th day of consecutive months astonished everyone.

The girls' memories now inevitably became intertwined with Alan's story. The trips to town on Fridays but especially 'Evanseezade', their name for the store that sold bottled lemonade, or if they were really good they were allowed a 'Spider' (a fancy glass of lemonade with a scoop of ice-cream and a paper straw). What a treat. During the winter months, the family, all dressed in woollen coats and fluffy woollen beanies knitted by Mavis, would sometimes travel into Corrigin with Alan to watch him play football.

Although footy had been more his pre-marriage pastime, he did occasionally fill in when needed. The car was parked on the edge of the playing field and the family watched from inside the car. But not realising their daughters were all short-sighted, Mavis and Alan didn't know the girls could not see Alan once he ran onto the field, so most of the focus was distinctly inside the car with its steamy windows creating drawing opportunities.

*The Corrigin football team. Back row: Bert Parsons (third from right) and Alan Parsons (second from right) and Donny Fulwood (front row, second from right)*

During the summer and after the harvest, the family would travel, initially to Mandurah for a beachside vacation. Visiting the beach after the long harvest was something most Wheatbelt families attempted to do. Many of the 1950s children of parents who holidayed like this, found their way to coastal living as adults. After 1957, the Parsons family went to Bunbury, to stay in a caravan on Hands Oval along with another farming family, the Smiths.

*Julie, Mavis and Eleanor at Mandurah for the 'after the harvest' break, 1956*

Mavis Horner in 1948

CHAPTER SIX

# *"This multi-talented, creative being is such a mystery"*
## *Yvonne Matthews*

## *All about Mavis*

Mavis was a conundrum from the start. She not only performed the domestic duties required to support her hardworking husband, but overcame the solitude that came her way with the isolation of 1950s farm life. Mavis was after all a town girl from a close family.

## *Overcoming isolation*

The most consistent activity by Mavis, and her ever-increasing number of children, was to listen to Kindergarten of the Air and try to follow the useful suggestions, but it was Catherine King's ABC Women's Session on the wireless, between 9.45 and 11.30 am every morning that fed her the mental nutrients she needed.

The background behind the morning wireless programs deserves some consideration, for they were the lifeline for many a woman and her children for some 30 years, no matter where they lived. It all began in 1942 in Western Australia, when Catherine King started the soon-to-become nationwide Kindergarten of the Air. The little program and its far-reaching possibilities went on to be heard throughout the immediate Commonwealth countries (even soldiers overseas in Asia listened). It appears that during the war Kindergartens in Perth were closed, due to the potential threat of Japanese bombing. Catherine, in her wisdom and being a trained Kindergarten teacher, saw a way to remedy the loss and managed to get the ABC in Perth interested in transmitting a small, 20-minute program for the benefit of the affected children — it went viral, so to speak. The eastern states and ultimately those Commonwealth nations closest to Australia picked it up.

In an interview with King, carried out by Alison Gregg for her 1993 paper, *The hope of the future: The Kindergarten Union and the campaign for children's libraries in Western Australia*, Alison Gregg calls Catherine King a godsend to country women. Catherine was aware that in times of need, the wireless was very powerful. This developed an understanding of the difficulties faced by women and children in remote areas. The program she initiated, Kindergarten of the Air, became a valued support for many isolated children in the outback Wheatbelt.

According to Alison's interview with Catherine this was soon followed by the ABC Women's Session, which provided invaluable discussions ranging from parenting to science and from the arts to cooking. Music and live interviews were also included and catered to the needs of intelligent women who, although they were not in the paid workforce, were interested, thinking people with genuine concerns of their own.

Catherine King, who began her women's program in 1944, inspired Mavis in the most wondrous ways. For reasons known only to herself, Mavis set the goal of making the full suite of marionettes for the puppet show of *Peter and the Wolf*. The orchestral storytelling record was played to her daughters as they grew and each year she completed a little more of the complement of puppets.

*Puppet made by Mavis c.1956, Grandfather, from 'Peter and the Wolf'*

## The making of puppets

Mavis melted lead sinkers (then used as weights in the hems of curtains) in the firebox of her copper. The copper, fortunately, was in one of the outhouses and was normally used for boiling the washing. The molten lead was poured into moulds to become the weight needed for the sole of the puppet's shoes, thus keeping them grounded while the strings were active. She used plasticine to model their faces, then layered papier-mâché over this, finally bringing them to life with a painted face. Wool or corn silk was dried and glued on as hair or a beard. As her father and grandfather worked with wood in their back shed, so did she in her kitchen.

Mavis was no stranger to handling and manufacturing small wooden objects. She cut and carved and fitted the timber required for the legs, arms, hips and chest and used leather and fabric held in place with panel pins, adding eyelets for the strings. The hands were made from wire and covered in papier-mâché and then painted, thus allowing them to be bent to grasp an object if needed. Small garments were sewn and created to complete the image. Stringing the puppet was slow and measured but she accomplished the task. Her first complete character was the 'Grandfather'.

In other acts of inspiration, old tea chests were painted with beautiful images of toys climbing into them, a cue for the girls to put away their few toys perhaps. Curtains, tablecloths, pot holders, linen, frills and covers were sewn to put on painfully plain furniture and bare windows; overalls and frilly dresses with matching panties were made for the girls, not to mention the few beautifully tailored garments Mavis made for herself. With a single wardrobe between them and a quiet social life such exquisite clothing seldom made an appearance.

## *The maternity girls*

Mavis couldn't be described as having close friends but did have the odd social but meaningful encounter with two sisters, Shirley and Betty Steenson (Betty was her bridesmaid). As it turned out, as often was the case in those days, once the Steenson girls married farmers themselves, maintaining their friendship became more difficult, save for the respite spent in the maternity ward at the Corrigin hospital.

*Betty Durstan (née Steenson)*  *Betty Smith*  *Yvonne Matthews*

But two other friends travelled a further distance because Alan kept in touch with the families: Betty Smith whom Mavis befriended, along with fellow thespian Yvonne Matthews, in the maternity ward. Yvonne Matthews had arrived in town as a young bride with her husband Bill who was the new Goldsbrough Mort stock agent. Alan and Bill had 'clicked', which in those days was fortunate for the wives because it offered more opportunity for social interaction. Yvonne explains this experience in an email she sent Julie in December 2016:

> *I can't really recall my first meeting with Queen Mavis. I am guessing it was in the usual manner of things in those days … If the new Goldsbrough Bloke had a missus she would be discreetly, and indiscreetly, checked out, assessed and put in a slot by the locals — the locals being those born in the district or at least those who went to school here — and even after 60+ years those criteria still have a bearing on one's placement. So I guess during that vetting process we came to know each other, probably via the maternity ward also intermittently, but the glue in the mix comes from the fellows. They obviously clicked early on and we touched base on the boundary, when convenient.*

## An element of the theatrical

At one stage Mavis briefly joined the local Repertory Club with her like-minded friend Yvonne. Yvonne also wrote of the experience in the Repertory Club and then went on to describe how their loose, but solid friendship had survived into the 21st century:

> *Mavis was so accomplished it amazed me, her talents were applauded and aided and abetted by Alan — encouragement it is called — while my extra attempts at out of home activities were always met with suspicion and amateur dramatics. However, the Rep. Club, that was our common ground. Mavis was a remarkable talent in such valuable ways: costumes, artistically, musical expertise. Just a wonderful asset. My most 'gob-smacking' memories of her*

*were her sculpture and above all her marionettes. All the while we were populating Corrigin. I humbly say this, but for the first time in my life I felt I had found a kindred spirit. Nowadays, our brief touching of base on rare and distant occasions, we just slip into a slot that lies there, dormant and waiting ... and we enter a zone ... private and ours and comfortable. Wit and silliness abound and it is OK coz it is us. Even her relocation to Bunbury changed nothing, our singular lives didn't merge, we went our separate ways but whenever the twain met, there we were again, in our zone!*

As Yvonne says she has long puzzled over Mavis and her abilities. These are her ponderings written in a follow up email later in December 2016:

*Precious Jules. Isn't it amazing, intriguing, sad that this multi-talented creative being is such a mystery. I have long puzzled over her background, the quality of the birthright that bestowed such incredible artistic ability upon her. I mean, this is not just an ability to sing, hold a tune or sew a fine seam or paint a stick figure picture to amuse a child, it is much, much more than that. There was/is an incredible depth/perfection. The singing was the musical expression and of course the making of the sound, physically playing an instrument.*

*Who encouraged/financed her teachers? We all came from times of meagre financial means, most of us, it wouldn't have been common or probably easy. Her parents must have had similar ability in their background to impose such extras into a small girl's curricula. It was as if she had a deeper, stronger psyche, that absorbed basic info and developed it 'to the nth degree'. Sculpting/ puppet making/exclusive needle craft, this isn't some blessed soul of special gifted tutelage, in my knowing a basic farm wife, bowed to the weather wiles and work men calling the shots, intermittently presenting yet another child.*

*We were a breed lost in many ways methinks and sadly this silly semi-theatrical, nonsensical friendship we were so delightfully allowed seems, in hindsight, to have been superficial, just us sailing along in the moment not indulging in why or wherefore.*

# Talents fostered

Yvonne's puzzlement raises many questions about how Mavis acquired her skill set. When asked, Mavis recalled her days at West Leederville Primary School in Woolwich St, and that every Tuesday she would go to a music lesson on the way home, a few streets from the school. Her teacher, a chubby little old lady, taught young Mavis at her house. Apparently, Mavis's mother received some money after the death of her first husband Clement Wood, which she then used to pay for Mavis's music lessons. After the lesson Mavis would continue on home to Wembley, sometimes catching a ride with her father on his way home from work on the railway. Mavis's daughter, Susan, tells the tale:

> *She remembers running like the wind all the way to the piano lesson and when done would run with delight to Cambridge Street. She knew every garden wall, street curb, bush and pavement crack and would leap and bound over obstacles with sure-footed abandon. She felt like she was flying and loved the feeling. If she ran really fast, she would be in time to meet her dad at the top of the hill. He rode a man's tall bike and he would hoist her up onto the handlebars and dink her home. It was one of the rare moments of joyous companionship between them both. It was also a rare time when he let her borrow his bike and she would wheel it up to the top of Essex St (they lived in number 10), clamber up onto the crossbar and then let gravity do the rest as she whizzed down the hill, sitting side saddle, with the wind in her face and feeling an unrestrained freedom.*

Mavis told how unique her Wednesdays were, with a curious practice Mavis considered a treat. She would return home at lunch-time to have a special lunch with her mother. To do this, little Mavis would have to run down Northwood Street to catch a trolley bus in Cambridge Street to her Essex Street home, about 24 streets on. When she arrived, she would change into a clean dress, which was laid out on her bed for her, and then sit down to a special lunch with her mother. After which she would have to repeat the procedure in reverse to return to school for the afternoon lessons. The understanding about why this happened this way is long since lost so we can but speculate. Perhaps some special fresh produce was only available at that time or this happened after wash day or perhaps it was music lesson day?

*Mavis with her father in his Cameron Highlander's uniform kilt 1936.*

*From its inception in 1936, 16th Battalion - The Cameron Highlanders of WA - wore a tartan originally adopted in 1794 by the newly raised 79th Regiment in Scotland, which later became the Queen's own Cameron Highlanders. The Cameron Highlanders are still active in WA today.*

## *So why was Mavis so accomplished at sewing, painting, piano, singing, dancing?*

Mavis's mother, Annie, like her father before her, played the violin while other family members were able to play the piano well; her mother and grandfather could play a tune brilliantly — by ear. Mavis's daughter Susan shares her observations:

*Somewhere along the way Mavis had piano lessons from an obviously very good teacher who imparted to her an ability to sight-read with exactness as well as an appreciation of the classics.*

Mavis was also given a number of ballet lessons which is very apparent when you see the pose Mavis has adopted at every photo shoot since. She places one foot out in front with an elegant angle of the knee and ankle; giving her a model-like appearance.

*Annie, Wally, Ann, and Mavis in ballet pose watching Wally's dog called Peter c.1934*

All about Mavis

*Annie Hall, Mavis's mother, with her violin, (she was able to play by ear) c.1906*

According to Mavis, her mother and grandmother were keen and accomplished painters (of gentle pictures, says her cousin June), so it seemed second nature for her to pick up a pencil and paintbrush and start creating her own artistic endeavours.

Annie was 24 when she arrived in Australia but seemed to have already had some lessons in painting in Stockport, UK. There are still a number of her works scattered about the family. On occasion, she innovatively retouched monochromatic portrait photographs by painting into them with oils, of all things. Amongst the other pictures are a small quantity of studies of various flowers, a gypsy camp with fires burning in the forest and an American Indian girl drinking from a stream.

*Portrait of Annie Horner which she coloured in with oil paints, 1912*

# The fascinating Uncle Wally

Mavis's Uncle Wally was also a proficient artist, who encouraged not only Mavis but also her children in their artistic endeavours. Wally and most of the family members possessed a diabolical sense of humour, which was long since bestowed on Mavis. She adored this adventurous gentleman who made his money from a claim on the edge of The Golden Mile in Kalgoorlie/Boulder very early in life, and was able to pursue his other worldly interests. Wally had trained in design in Britain prior to setting sail to Australia, only to abruptly leave again in 1915 on board a ship bound for war-torn Egypt.

Corporal Wally Hall aged 21, in the army WA, 1915

The young adventurer, Wally Hall, who encouraged the family to come to WA

Three years after the war, his sisters Annie (then a chemist's assistant), and her husband Clement Wood (a chemist), Ethel (a photographer's assistant) with husband Sydney (a Cheshire newspaper journalist), set sail for Fremantle, Australia. They were followed by their sister Louie, who later was the only one to return to the UK.

It is understood Walter Hall (Wally) came to Western Australia towards the end of his teens. We don't yet know why. Wally began his career as an apprentice designer at a calico manufacturer in Stockport, UK. It is unclear when he left but it was after Annie's marriage to Clement. He was certainly in Western Australia when war broke out, so he joined the Australian army in Perth in 1915 stating his profession as shearer, of all things.

During the war, there is evidence he fought in Egypt and France and he travelled back and forth to the UK on leave from the army. This is when Wally began a relationship with his mother's cousin, Lillie Moult (Lillie's father was Joseph Crampton Moult, who married Ann Leah in 1874). Family comment holds that Lillie, born in 1885, was considered queen-like with pretensions to royalty in the way she conducted herself. She was indeed very proper. But she was not the only aspiring Royal.

Lillie and her cousin Ann (Mavis's grandmother), had bad feelings towards each other from then on, but despite the tension they all came to Australia in 1919-20, with Wally's prompting of course.

Wally chose to go prospecting and found a gold mine on the edge of The Golden Mile, while others in the family chose the more secure option of government assisted farming and lost everything. Wally certainly struck it rich — so rich that he stopped working at the age of 33, frequently travelling abroad for lavish holidays. He and Lillie lived in a three-storey house in Cottesloe, where he created 'inventions' in the basement. Unbelievably some were utilised in WWII, but these remain top secret to this day.

However, prospecting ended when a dispute occurred between Wally (with his partners) and the wealthy gold financier and businessman, Claude de Bernales (who built London Court in 1937, in Perth's city centre). According de Bernales' on-line biography, by John H. Laurence:

*His most prestigious coup came in 1936 when he won control of Great Boulder Proprietary Gold Mine, one of the oldest and richest mines of the 'Golden Mile'.*

As the owner of the Golden Mile, Claude de Bernales had accused Wally and the team of entering a vein, which was supposedly rightfully part of the de Bernales claim, The Golden Mile. The whole thing was fought out in the Courts. The location of Claude de Bernales' family home (now the Cottesloe Civic Centre) made them neighbours. Wally lived in the street behind it. June, Mavis's cousin, remembers Wally giving her his binoculars to observe what was happening in the de Bernales backyard. What is not told in de Bernales' biography is that Wally's team, John Stene, William Robertson and William Graunte, challenged Claude's 1936 coup in the High Court and had a partial win in 1937. Wally and Lillie continued living on the finance gained, staying in Cottesloe until around 1949 when they moved to a home on the Swan River in Belmont.

*Lillie and Wally Hall whilst on one of their many trips abroad c.1940s*

## *Wally to the rescue*

With the rest of the family in financial difficulty, Wally found he was unable to accommodate his struggling parents, James and Ann, in his own home because his mother and his wife Lillie could not, or would not, speak to each other. Wally solved the problem by building on single rooms at both his sisters' simple homes.

The little Wembley house was where Mavis (b.1926) and her parents, Bill and Annie, and Mavis's half-sister Nancy lived, while Ethel's Inglewood home already housed her husband Sydney Mansell and daughter June (b.15 June1929).

The plan was that the grandparents, Ann and James, would live six months alternately with each of their daughters, Annie and Ethel. It appears Wally's other sister, Louie had previously returned to the UK, her departure somewhat a mystery.

Ethel & Sydney Mansell with daughter June, at their home in Inglewood, 1942

Annie Wood (née Hall) with her daughter Nancy c.1918 (hand coloured by Annie)

All about Mavis

*Louie Walker née Hall c.1918*

# The elusive Auntie Louie

Louie was an excellent dressmaker and often made dolls from old stockings. She made one such doll for Mavis. The ringlets in the hair are meticulously made from a combination of lace work and crochet. The doll still remains in the family.

Louie's mother, Ann Hall, had a passion for the exquisite, possibly in keeping with the perceived regal status. She owned a Queen Anne chaise longue, which took pride of place in the Ord Street house in Claremont that they occupied in their later years.

This object was revered and family members knew never to use it casually, all except Louie's husband Charles Walker that is. Charles was a

*Doll made by Louie from old stockings shaped and filled with kapok. Note the lace-work for the hair.*

widower with a baby son Leslie, whom Louie raised. Charles made a big mistake the day he discreetly lay down his head in the solitude of the sitting room. But the chaise longue, being encumbered with a lower arm at its end, soon saw his long legs dangle over its silken covered, delicately carved, timber. The discovery of this large undignified man draped over her prize possession created an incident with undreamt of repercussions. An argument broke out between family members over the disrespect shown by Charles. Mavis remembers Louie, Charles and his son Leslie setting off on board ship for a supposed holiday to the Orient. But they never came back. It is believed they returned to England.

Years later, June remembers her Grandma Hall being very, very attached to her antique chaise longue. She says when Grandma Hall moved to live with the Mansells the chaise longue came too and assumed pride of place in the lounge room. June says it had tassels on the bottom of the upholstery and her pug dog kept appearing with a tassel in his mouth!

## *The Elegant Ethel*

When you knocked at her door you needed to be prepared to wait, as the elegantly dressed Ethel flurried about opening doors and windows and stubbing out her cigarette, which of course she never smoked! Housework done and dressed in her finest she was ready to receive. Her quiet husband Sydney, a gentle man, had found work better suited to him, as personal secretary to the chief administrator and Lord Mayor for the City of Perth. In Stockport, Ethel retouched black and white photographs with the most delicate hints of colour, in Inglewood she transformed into homemaker extraordinaire, fulfilling her little family's needs with superb culinary skills. She and her sister Annie would embark on shopping trips to the city despite a lack of any sense of direction. Exiting from a department store lift, in fits of laughter but completely lost, they would entertain their daughters June and Mavis and many more to boot. Eventually the giggling group would arrive for an afternoon tea of cake and buns at Foy's cafeteria.

## *Railway transfer to the seaside town of Bunbury*

Mavis and her parents left Wembley after her father's transfer with the railways. They moved to Beach Road in Bunbury, where teenager Mavis continued her piano lessons at the Convent of Mercy in the town centre. Once her schooling at the Convent began, it also included singing lessons. When she was thirteen she began to learn shorthand, and typing from Sister Mary Paul and by fourteen she had graduated from the Convent having completed a bookkeeping course. This enabled Mavis to procure a job in the office at the Bunbury Hospital in the town centre (where the library now stands).

Mavis learned to sew at school and helped out with the mending at home. Her family were not well off so Mavis learnt the art of repair and how to create the fantastic from very little. Her grandmother and mother were also adept at lace-making, but it didn't stop there.

*Ethel Mansel née Hall c.1912*

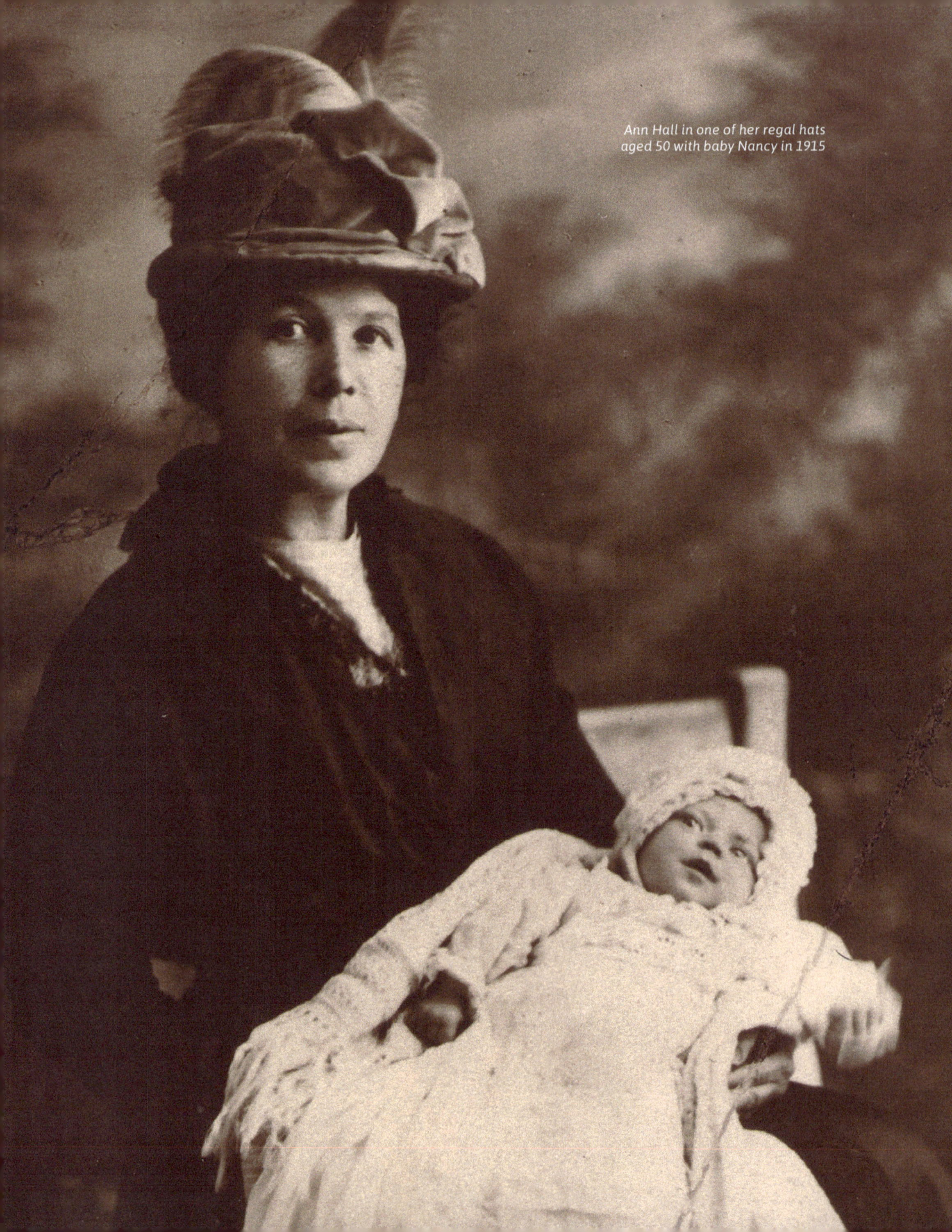
Ann Hall in one of her regal hats aged 50 with baby Nancy in 1915

# *A word about hats*

Mavis's grandmother Ann had millinery skills, which she applied to make hats for herself and her family. She was driven by her admiration for Queen Mary and would recreate the latest millinery styles the Queen wore.

This is no surprise when you learn of her connections back in London. Mavis's grandmother, Ann Hall (née Moult) had a brother, John Moult, who, when he married Elizabeth Keogh in 1908, moved in with her family to both live and work in Carnaby Street, London. The address is significant because this was where the Keogh family of dressmakers and tailors proudly made garments for the Royal family.

*John Moult Snr.*

John Moult Snr. (1839-1903) married Phoebe Marsland (1836-1919) in 1860. Father to Joseph (1860-68); Hannah (1864-1908); Ann (1865-1949); Mary Alice (1869-1974); John Moult (1872-1957); Emma (1875 -?); and four infant deaths. Phoebe gave birth to eleven babies in total.

Another vital clue to her acquisition of millinery skills was that Ann's husband James was described in the 1911 Census as a felt hatter in 1911, at Stockport, UK. Stockport is well known for its tradition in the centuries-old textile and hat making industries and was considered Britain's centre for these artforms.

# The further enigma of Grandfather James Hall

Interestingly, James' father's ancestors were involved with the iconic Bramall Hall in Stockport, UK. The Halls lived in the gatehouse when the Davenport family lived at Bramall Hall, and with their staff and others, worked to make it a self-sufficient estate. The Davenports were the lords of the Manor for 500 years. As 'Hall' is James's surname it is not hard to consider the probability his family were involved for a significant period (although to date this is unproven). James's family occupied the gatehouse. The Davenports sold the 2,000-acre estate in 1877 when James would have been a young boy and the Hall family moved on.

*Bramall Hall gatehouse where James Hall lived as a child with his family until 1877*

In 1881, James was apprenticed to a joiner, which no doubt gave him skills to make timber hat blocks, onto which felt hats were formed. However, by 1891 he was married to Ann and working as a rail clerk, living next door to his beloved parents

Samuel and Emma Hall (née Whiston b.1841). In 1901, he became a general labourer, before moving into the hatters industry, possibly at Battersby's Hat Factory in Stockport, first working as a hat body overlocker and then rising to become a foreman by 1914. Sadly, WWI changed Stockport by cutting off all the overseas markets to the port city, and 700 years of marketplace activity vanished overnight, eroding Stockport's eminence.

Ann Moult married James Hall in 1886 (registered in the March quarter), but their eldest daughter Annie was born on 18 February 1886, so it may have been a solution to a problem. Ann and James went on to have three more children, Ethel, Louise (Louie) and John Walter (Wally).

On the night of the UK 1911 Census they were all at 6 Southwood Rd, Stockport, just off Buxton Rd. Through photographic evidence it appears possible that Louie (1890-1970) returned from Australia to the area where she had grown up, though this is not verified as yet.

## *Why was everyone leaving the UK again?*

Ann and James Hall embarked at London Docks on the Orsova on 22 November 1919, arriving in Fremantle on 26 December 1919, making them the first of the family to arrive in Western Australia as permanent residents. The decision to come to WA rested with Wally, their enterprising son, who had previously been to Perth just as WWI broke out and had joined up in Perth. Wally returned with his new wife Lillie in 1920 (though they were supposed to come on an earlier ship but their passage was cancelled).

Conditions in the UK early in the 20th century were indeed trying. WWI had left its mark bringing many changes to industry and living conditions. The economy was in trouble because funding the war had put Britain into severe debt; Britain, a powerful and worldly nation, had never been attacked like that and experienced a sense of vulnerability from the bombs and poisonous gas that were dropped. The war also left Britain in a state of social trauma and to top it all, there was an influenza epidemic.

*ill vi: Graphite drawing (detail) taken from early 1900s postcard image of Boots Chemist, Windsor*

Women who had entered the industrial workforce during the war were now stronger in both numbers and intent, with movements towards equality. Many countries in the Commonwealth also stood tall and displayed their own nationalism, expressed in eagerness to be free of Britain's constraints. Developments in medical technology changed the way medicines were produced, to treat new health conditions and injuries that emerged as a consequence of the war.

Just why the exodus of the entire Hall family took place is probably due to economic factors. The immediate and obvious one for Annie and Clem was that Boots was sold by Jesse Boots in 1920 to the American United Drug Company. At that stage, Boots was a herbal medicine shop. Things were about to change with the advent of new American medicines discovered during the war, and no doubt this threat required different skill sets, which undermined Clement's profession.

# *Mavis's grandparents James and Ann Hall in Perth*

Ann is described as 'wilful and stately', and as living in a world of her own (possibly as she aligned herself with Queen Mary). Ann painted and was a skilled milliner; she applied herself to various craft pursuits and became adept at most arts and crafts of the time. In her later years, she made exquisite dolls using papier-mâché to make the heads and limbs or she would make them from old socks and stockings, all finished and dressed in beautifully made outfits. These were donated to children in need. Ann always conducted a morning constitutional walk about the garden before she started her day. She walked everywhere, often impatiently between trolley stops until the trolley bus caught up with her, which made her very fit.

Their granddaughter, Mavis, described James as a chatty, playful fellow who talked to her far more than her Grandmother Ann ever did. James attempted to teach Mavis Esperanto, believing it to be the new universal language. James was dark-eyed and apparently his mother (Emma Whiston) had black eyes. Her ancestors were barge people who used horses to pull a barge along the river. James could certainly play a fine tune on the violin without need of sheet music. Mavis enjoyed him. He was always able to ease any tension at the dinner table. At one stage James built an extraordinary chair from bush branches exposing his creative mind.

*Mavis aged six*

Perhaps he built the chair from the branches of the same tree which captured little Mavis by her panties as she scaled its heights. Climbing trees in a frock was never easy but the humiliation of being caught by your underwear was memorable.

Ann and James Hall on a bridge in parklands (notice the detail in Ann's hat) c.1910

Firmly attached to a branch high above the ground and needing her father to climb up and release her and the said garment, was cause for great family humour for years to come.

Once in Perth, somewhere along the way James found work at the Swan Brewery.

In those days workers were permitted and even encouraged to drink the beer, which may have resulted in him becoming an alcoholic, or as believed and often said by family 'the alcohol affected his brain' not to mention the lightning strike. Mavis describes a story about her grandfather revealing a strange event, which changed him forever. Certainly, the adults in the family thought so. James was sitting on a rocking chair in a corner of the kitchen of their home at 45 Ord Street, Claremont, when a bolt of lightning struck the house directly above where he sat. It visibly jolted him across the room. The family group all saw the event, no doubt because they were inclined to stay close.

## *Staying close*

Back in the mid-1920s, after Clem Wood drowned in the dam and the Kondinin farming enterprise folded, the sisters and their families were left with next to nothing. As the story goes they first lived all together in McCourt Street, Subiaco, the street where the old Subiaco fire station was located. This may have been where Ann and James were living in the 1920s, as they did not go to Kondinin with the others.

In May 1926, Annie, who was pregnant with Mavis, married Bill (William Horner) at the Methodist Manse Church, Cambridge Street, West Leederville, barely one month before Mavis was born in June 1926. Bill had just turned 24 a couple days beforehand but Annie was already 40. Bill had been on the Kondinin property employed to ringbark, fell and burn the trees in an effort to clear the land, as part of the group's commitment to the Western Australian government. Later, in 1928, Ann and James Hall's daughter Ethel, and her husband Sydney Mansell, found a home at 195 Sixth Avenue, Inglewood.

## *William Horner explained*

William (Bill) was born in 1902, apparently in Edinburgh, the illegitimate child of Inspector Norris (of Hull Street Police, now known as Humberside Police in Yorkshire). The family believe he may have also worked at Scotland Yard.

Bill's mother Emma had been Norris' housekeeper and when she fell pregnant with Norris' child, she left in shame, but soon married a farmer named Horner, who kindly gave Bill his name. In wedlock, Emma had more children but went on to marry another man called Simpson and had even more children. Bill's background is sketchy but we know he was made to work hard on the Simpson farm, owned a kilt and played soccer, and had come to Australia with his half-brother, Walter R. Norris alias Dobby Norris. It is said they came out 'below decks'. Bill gave his birth father's surname to Mavis as her second name, Mavis Norris Horner.

Bill Horner's brother Walter (Dobby) Norris. The policemen at Hull Street Station c.1912

*Bill Horner's father, Inspector Norris of Hull Street Police Station c.1900*

Bill Horner's mother, Emma Simpson at work on
the Simpson farm (she married Harry Simpson) c.1917

Bill Horner's mother, Emma, UK 1957, in her
late 60s, a similar age to Bill's wife Annie

The brother was a policeman, confirmed by a photograph that Mavis saw many times, showing her Uncle Dobby standing amongst a tiered group of policemen back in the UK. Dobby apparently was somewhat older than Bill. His wife was always referred to as Aunty Norrie, a nickname like Dobby's. Once in WA, the Norris couple lived their days on a farm in Yearling but had no children. The question of exactly how Bill formed a relationship with his half-brother, the son of the man who had his way with the young maid, Bill's mother, is a riddle. She may have been 'upstairs' at the time but she had to leave via the downstairs backdoor.

Bill was probably very comfortable with his wife Annie being considerably older than he, possibly because he strived for a relationship with his mother who appeared to suffer no shortage of men and children in her life. Annie may have been able to give him the sense of a mother's love he possibly craved at times ... perhaps?

By 1929, Annie, her new husband Bill, her eleven-year-old daughter Nancy and baby Mavis had found a home at 10 Essex St Wembley.

*Horner family home, 10 Essex Street Wembley WA. The corner store across the road was where Mavis was sent to purchase her sister's cigarettes c.1939*

# *A little madness*

After 1937, as has been suggested, things got tough for their parents, James and Ann, and it was agreed that Ethel and Annie would share responsibility for them by taking turns to provide accommodation at each other's homes every six months. But James and Ann only spent their first half year as a couple with Annie and Bill in Wembley. Mavis remembers James would spend hours doing woodwork in the back shed. Mavis liked visiting the shed where she would watch both her father and grandfather at work.

Care of the parents occurred this way despite the fact that Ann's son Wally had a veritable mansion at the beachside suburb of Cottesloe. Grandmother Ann could not accept the fact that her cousin Lillie had married her son (some nine years younger than her). Tragically for Wally and Lillie in those days it was advised not to have children as the blood line was close.

With the bedsit freshly built at Essex Street, Ann and James moved into their own small area. The new room was a source of great pleasure but an argument between them broke out when Ann decided she wanted to hang a painting. To James this meant defacing the beautiful build. Ann's determination to hang her adored painting ultimately caused James to lash out, whereupon he grabbed the hammer from her and simply hit her on the head. This caused a revolution in the house. James was captured, dispatched into Mavis's bedroom and locked in. Thereafter he was locked in that room during the night. He was always heard pleading with Bill to let him out.

As the family genuinely believed he wanted to harm Ann, he was assigned to an old men's home on the cliffs overlooking the Swan River in Nedlands/Dalkeith. Its location may have seemed perfect but the conditions were not pristine. All this confused Mavis, as she could not see him as a threat. She thought they had all gone mad. Visits were stiff and uncomfortable with his constant pleading to be taken home. His head was shaved because he caught lice and he continually said he was starving and grew thinner and thinner. According to Mavis, her Granddad James was very sad and simply died in April 1941.

It broke Mavis's heart. He was always her ally against her older half-sister, Nancy, who perpetually demanded and bullied Mavis to do certain chores for her. Many a time when Mavis was seated, poised ready for her beloved evening radio serial, Nancy would command her to quickly buy a pack of cigarettes. Mavis soon learnt objection had a price so made the chore into a racing game. She measured her stealth by how quickly she could run across the road to the corner deli, make her purchase and be back in time for the start. The glamorous Nancy was always whispering and plotting with her mother, Annie, chiefly about the shortcomings of the men folk in the house. Mavis felt Nancy was never far from trouble between people in the house.

*Glamourous Nancy Wood c.1936*

# The charming Nancy Gray

Mavis' half-sister was eleven years older and knew a thing or two about the ways of the world long before Mavis was out of bobby socks. Mavis had to do as she was told. Nancy's beautiful (enhanced) red hair, forceful nature and strong intelligence made her someone to be reckoned with, and to behold.

In 1942, Nancy married Jack Collins but with World War II in full swing, Jack was sent to Darwin, where the Japanese were bombing Australia. When he came home on leave he suffered trauma-related depression; meanwhile Nancy lived in their flat in Perth's city centre and was enjoying a completely different life style. She worked on the first floor in Boan's, a city department store, as head girl in fine china and kitchenware and thus possessed a degree of independence.

By 1946, for whatever reason, Nancy filed for divorce and Jack took full responsibility, or so it appeared on paper, claiming to have had relations with another woman on the 5th of January that year. This type of admission was how a divorce could be procured in the 1940s. In reality Nancy had met a USA serviceman, Lieutenant John Hamilton. However, he had returned to the USA at the end of the war in 1945, believing Nancy would follow to become his wife once she was able to sort out her papers. A visa was needed and her immigration papers. Nancy's divorce came through in September of 1946, and so did her visa application. But, in the meantime, Nancy continued to enjoy a rich social life and had met a distinguished WA doctor. Sadly, John Hamilton was still writing and living in hope about her immigration in April 1947.

Finally, the crunch came and Nancy packed her bags and went to the airport to fly out to America. But she didn't board the plane. A gallant, and smitten Dr Allan Gray retrieved her before she boarded. Nancy too must have had strong feelings for the doctor because if she had wanted to leave, nothing would have stopped her.

In those days, it was considered disastrous for a distinguished doctor and gentleman to marry a divorcee, so they hatched a plan. They discreetly went to live in Tasmania where Nancy changed her name by deed poll from Collins to Gray on the 7th of May 1947. She had borne two children (Hilton and Kimbal) before she finally married Allan Gray some ten years later, in 1957.

*Nancy, bridesmaid at a friend's wedding, with flower girl Mavis c.1936*

*Ann Hall reading in the garden c.1945*

## *Grandma Hall's end*

Bill's work on the railways took him and his family to Bunbury towards the end of the 1930s, by which time Nancy had already left home, leaving Ethel and Sydney to care for Ann.

Toward the end of Ann's life, she lived in the small room at her daughter Ethel's home in Inglewood. Here she continued to make her papier-mâché dolls with their beautiful hand-painted faces, each exquisitely clothed. It is said she simply wore out, dying peacefully two days after Ethel's 61st birthday in October 1949. But in reality, according to the death certificate, she died from arteriosclerosis.

## *Over the Moon with June*

*June and Brian during their courtship days c.1950*

June, a smart young thing, won a scholarship to Perth Modern and then marched right into teachers' college and into the arms of fellow student Brian McGinnity whom she married in 1951. Together they became intrepid educators in little schools in remote Western Australian country towns. Nevertheless, June produced four children; Anne, Pat, Shane and Terry, all, due to these isolated situations, learning a kind of self-reliance as a family. By the time secondary education was on the agenda the family had relocated to Kalamunda, where June and Brian nestled into the comfort of a strong community made all the more stable by their presence in it.

## *Back to Mavis*

Mavis's endeavours, her enquiring mind, and her belief in her abilities to recreate things she liked, were well fuelled by her ancestral family. As with all things creative, inspiration is the ignition and Mavis possessed plenty of that. Although she kept a modest half-a-dozen books yielding beautiful works of art and photographic captures of costumed movie stars on film sets, her tenacious ability to research and follow through meant she was never far from her own gathered 'how to' material. Notes from Catherine King's radio program, magazine cuttings, scribbles exploring garments and other inspiring objects were all kept. And on those days when time permitted, things happened. Even snatched moments playing a tune on her beloved piano, another vital tool of creative expression, fed her wellbeing.

*Mavis's daughters, Susan (in front), Eleanor and Julie
(dog kennel and sheds in distance) on the farm, 1958*

As with most 1950s, isolated women on farms, for Mavis, doing chores, caring for her industrious husband, and raising their daughters were always at the top of her agenda, but so too was her honesty in discovering and developing her own unique abilities, and in so doing she shone like a beacon for generations to come.

*Mavis and Peter, the dog, doing chores on the farm at Gorge Rock, 1950s*

# Part Three

## On thriving in Western Australia: Parsons in the South West

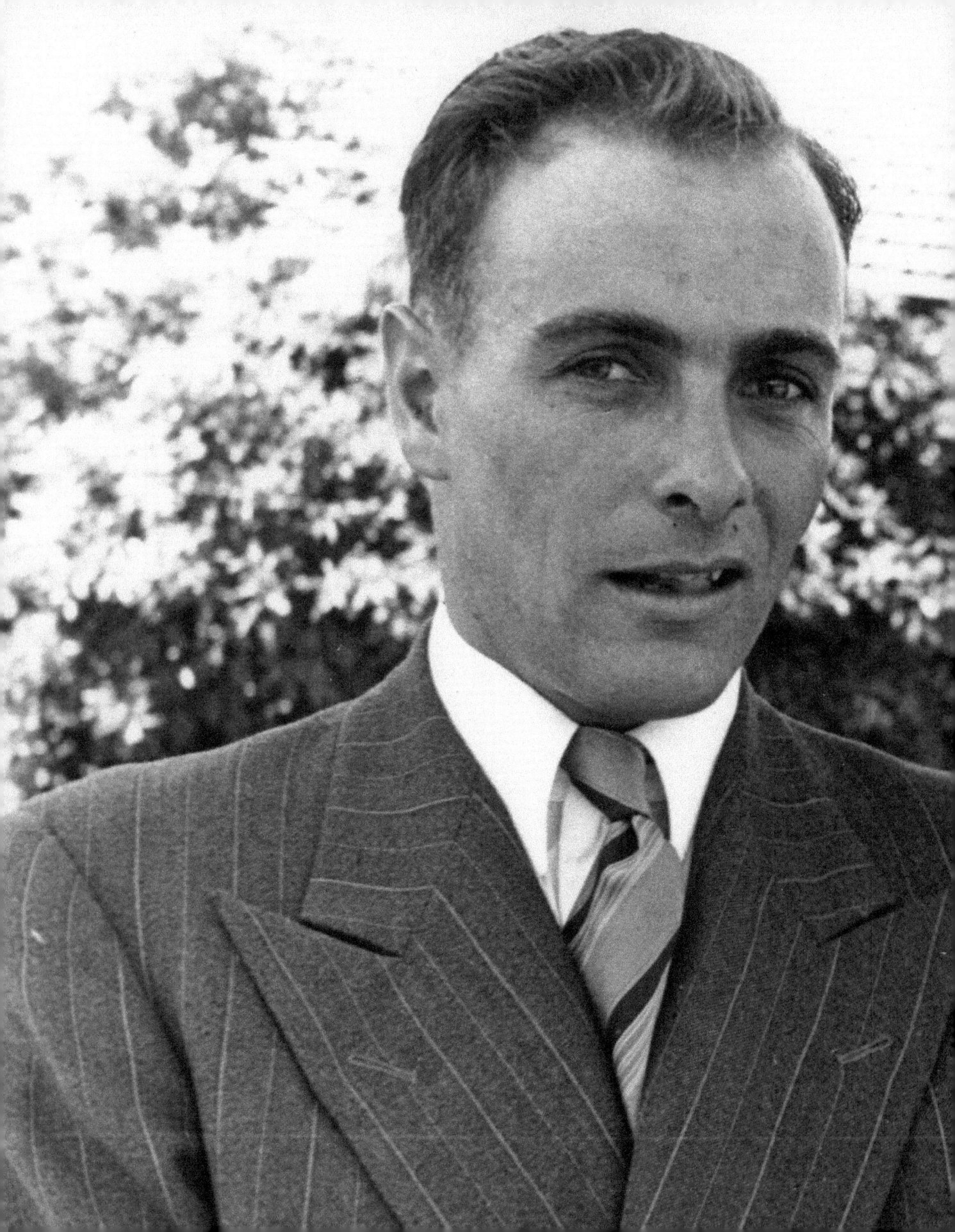

7:1 Mavis and Alan in 1950

*Caravans on Hands Oval. The Smiths and Parsons usually holidayed together after the harvest. Susan, Eleanor, & Julie Parsons with Suellen Smith 1959*

CHAPTER SEVEN

## *"Everything happens in 10-year cycles"*
### *Alan Parsons*

### *1959, a decision made*

When the decision was made to leave the farm, Alan asked Mavis where she thought they should go — she said Bunbury. Summer holidays in the town had enabled a certain sort of familiarity. Albany was also in the running but as Mavis had lived in Bunbury prior to moving to Corrigin, she was confident and comfortable with this decision.

In fact, the farm was sold while the family holidayed in Bunbury with the Smiths, after their 1959 harvest. Getting news of the sale to Alan took some effort on the part of his mate Bill Matthews. Thinking no-one would buy the farm Alan had nonchalantly listed it with Bill at Goldsbrough Mort.

Meanwhile the farming families had travelled to Bunbury for the summer break and had set up on Hands Oval. The Smiths owned a big white, maroon-striped, plywood van, which they towed to Bunbury, while Alan hired a caravan for Mavis and their excited girls. These two vans and about four others were parked under the trees on the low-lying corner of the park near where Blair Street roundabout now passes. It was shady and cool and the only place in Bunbury where you could park a van. There were simply no caravan parks in Bunbury in 1959 and this makeshift park did not even have an address, let alone a telephone. Faced with no alternative Bill Matthews sent a telegram: *'GOT RID OF YOU AT LAST YOU BASTARD (stop)'*

Alan rightly assumed that Bill had sold the property. With news of the sale in mind Alan and Mavis finished their holiday and returned to Corrigin to finalise the deal with the purchaser, the Hitchcock family. Once all that was completed they only had eight weeks to clear out all the farming equipment and stock. The usual procedure was to organise and hold a clearing sale. In addition, they had to pack up what they would need to start their new life and find a place they could move into upon their immediate arrival in Bunbury.

Within two weeks of the eight-week evacuation period before the big move, it was clear Mavis and the girls had to stay somewhere else if Alan was to achieve all that was before him. At this stage, the girls were aged six, four and two and needed all of Mavis's attention, making it difficult to pack the household up while they were all still ensconced. After careful negotiation, it was agreed Alan would take the family along with Peter the dog, to stay with Mavis's parents, who had since moved to Midland following another of Bill's transfers with work on the Railways.

That done, Alan had free rein to do it all his way. He admits to repairing and painting into the night for six weeks. When he had completed that part, he began to place everything to be sold in orderly rows from the shed to the pig sties, starting with tins of rusty nuts and bolts and all the accumulated tools and gear that farmers have, then onto the bigger machines, all and sundry.

In the middle of all that, Alan made appropriate arrangements enabling the family to make the transition to a new life in Bunbury. Getting somewhere to live was top of the list. Alan drove 300 kms to Bunbury and went into the first real estate agency he saw. Real estate agent Rodney Johnston happened to be in the front office at the time and helped Alan with the rental of a house. Unbeknown to them, a long friendship would follow. Alan then organised a removalist company to transport the household furniture.

# The sale

Goldsbrough Mort, and Alan's mate Bill Matthews, were the obvious choice for the auctioneers. Bill's boss and regional manager was Stan Magee, who had his management offices at Bruce Rock. Magee was an excellent auctioneer so Alan and Bill were pleased when he agreed to attend the sale.

*Bill Matthews (left), the sales rep for Goldsbrough Mort, with Corrigin farmers Ben Richardson, Alf Langford, Ralph Keys c.1959. After Alan left Corrigin, Bill resigned and became a successful farmer for the rest of his working life.*

On the day of the sale, Alan wasn't sure how it was going to work as he could see people all over the place looking at various items. After applauding Alan's layout, Magee politely enquired as to how he would like the sale to run, and with Alan's reply to simply 'commence', Magee casually walked over to the rusty nuts and bolts and began by yelling 'sale-o, sale-o'. The smart Magee had 'commenced' alright, but not in the way Alan had expected. He started by knocking all the prices right down. People ran from everywhere. Once he had command and the full attention of the crowd Magee skilfully brought up the prices. Alan's mate Bill also enjoyed the auctioneer's experience when he was able to take over from Magee, yielding some excellent results himself. Alan's precursor to his sales ability revealed itself that day. Alan says his greatest coup was his railway sleepers:

> I had about 500 railway sleepers to build more pig sties with. Realising no-one would buy so many in one hit, I stacked them into heaps of 50. I had bought them from the railways for £1 per one hundred but I had to pick them up from the railway line wherever they were and cart them home. The stacks of 50 averaged £50 each, so I was happy with such a workload being all worthwhile. The sheep, pigs and chooks were auctioned, while the grain, haystack, and the cow were sold separately. In fact, I was very proud of the result of the sale. Many people and the auctioneers congratulated me on such a successful sale.

On top of all that, the local ladies had banded together to create a wonderful atmosphere in the farmhouse. They had all worked hard to prepare and serve a brilliant afternoon tea appreciated by all. It was a dual-purpose delight with funds raised going to the Gorge Rock Pool.

## Patrick Street and a job

Rodney Johnston was indeed the very first person Alan met in 1959 when he arrived in Bunbury. Rodney was, among other things, an estate agent with Steere and Clarke, and had set the family up in a rented house at 11 Patrick Street for £2 a week.

Exhausted from the preceding two months of hard work, Alan had planned a month-long break in order to look around for work and settle in. This proved challenging when two weeks after their move to Bunbury, Alan was buying a bottle of beer to share with Mavis at the Highway Hotel. In the front bar, he bumped into John Dutton, whom he had known from Corrigin. Dutton was a zone manager for International Harvester and was having a drink with a bloke called Bill Dixon. Dixon was about to be appointed the dealer for International Harvester in Bunbury and he was casting around for staff. John had resigned from International Harvester to be the sales manager in the new Bunbury dealership. Given Alan's timely appearance, Dutton suggested Alan would make a good salesman.

This is because Alan possessed sound knowledge of farm machinery and had already proved himself to Dutton. When Dutton and the Corrigin International Harvester dealer visited Alan's farm a few years earlier, Alan managed to turn the tables on them and was selling them the concept of the new Fordson tractor cab. Alan, always an innovative thinker, was quick off the mark in purchasing a cab, which fitted onto the tractor offering the operator respite from the elements.

Mavis, never far from the front line, had worked at the Ford dealership affording a continuing, and beneficial, relationship where Alan, as a customer, reaped these benefits with good prices. Alan was one of the first to buy a tractor cab and after his many sunstroke events, with good reason. This made it easy for Alan to sell the cab concept to these two would-be-salesmen. Having failed to sell Alan a tractor, they left with something to think about in regard to the cab modification.

Alan, having found himself with a job offer, accepted and became a salesman with the Bunbury International Harvester Company dealership. The remuneration offered was £12 per week as a retainer, he was to run his own car, but would receive a two per cent commission on new products sold and three per cent commission on used product sold. These were the same terms as the International Harvester Company salesmen in Perth received.

Keen to try his hand at the challenge, Alan was given a price book, a bag full of International Harvester Company brochures, an order pad, a hire purchase pad and books. However, the hindrance of not knowing anyone, and trying to sell through the unknown trading name of R.W. & T.R. Dixon, proved a degree of difficulty, which might have turned anyone else around and out of the sales arena, but not Alan. It took six long weeks to make his first sale.

Alan tenaciously went out and knocked on farmer's doors. He enjoyed meeting new people, finding out how the South West farming industry operated and best of all he found the challenge exciting. He sold his first new truck, then the trade-in. By being out in the field and assessing what he saw, Alan soon realised there was a huge market out there. This man was like no other, he was not afraid of putting the extra hours in and things started to happen for him.

In the meantime, Bill Dixon, who drove a big American car, had bought a big home near the ocean, which indicated he had plenty of money. He was starting to show flamboyance in his attitude towards dealing with the public, by showing off whilst doing deals and making decisions that affected profitability. Like all businesses, the first two years are the test for survival.

As good fortune would have it, within a short period Alan was offered an opportunity to buy into an unequal partnership with his boss, Bill Dixon. Alan accepted and Bill remained 'the boss' for another four years. Alan explained the gradual demise towards the end of the four-year period:

*It was then that he asked me to form a partnership and as I had money from the sale of the farm, we became 50 percent owners. But he kept borrowing funds for other projects outside of the business. At the end of the first year, the partnership was in trouble financially. He started blaming me and offered to buy my share. A figure was set at nine thousand pounds sterling for my share, which I accepted. His problems then multiplied, as no bank would lend him funds so I offered to buy him out.*

But it doesn't end there, with more to follow. Alan continued to learn his lessons well, all the while forging his place in the world of farm machinery and meeting the needs of the farmers in the district.

## *The family and their first electric fridge*

Meanwhile, during winter and back on the home front, life in suburbia soon revealed the Patrick Street house, with its overgrown Geraldton-wax hedge, was nothing more than a small dark, damp house, with a new electric fridge. Sickness prevailed. Julie the eldest, then aged six, was enrolled in the nearby South Bunbury Primary School. It was walking distance and Mavis would bundle whomever she could into the pusher or attach any heroic walkers to a lead, and head off to walk her painfully shy eldest daughter to school. At first Mavis would meet Julie after school at the school gate until gradually it was on the street from the school or even at the corner of Patrick Street itself. This was more often than not due to the amount of sickness in the house at any one time. The mildewy environs of the Patrick Street house took its toll on toddler Susan and four-year-old Eleanor. With Alan and Julie missing, and no means of transport, Mavis was left to care for the often-unwell Susan and Eleanor in this dank house, for most of the day. The new electric fridge was of little comfort.

Peter, the ever-loyal family farm dog, was ultimately confined to life on a chain after experiencing a number of dog attacks: in those days dogs were permitted to roam freely, and frequently travelled in packs throughout the town. Peter pined and struggled to make sense of his new life. However, these rogue dogs attacked him whilst he was in his own yard on the chain. It was heartbreaking but eventually Alan made the hard decision to put him down. Not a sadder day had come to pass.

## *Mangles Street and Gail's arrival*

In 1960 Mavis was pregnant again; fortunately plans for a new house were already underway. A block of land in Mangles Street was chosen and builder Jack Best set about building a brand new, brick and tile, three-bedroom home. The family was able to move in that same year.

One evening in December, Alan got home in the nick of time to get Mavis to hospital for the birth of Gail, their fourth daughter (who like her sisters was also born on the eighth day). Not without incident though, as Alan was held up by a traffic policeman and had a speeding fine to sort out later. Baby Gail was brought home to their glorious, brand new home about ten days after the birth, and thus began a new chapter of family life. The home itself had everything and more.

*Parsons girls on their new front veranda with the pansies just showing their heads in the flower box surround c.1961*

The cement front veranda was encased by a brick flower box of pansies, embedded at a right angle and ending at the front steps, which led up to the bottle green, glossy front door with a press-button door chime. There were three glass panel doors, which (seldom) opened onto the veranda. White terylene curtains were fitted onto stretchy lengths of thin-coiled wire attached to eyelets embedded in the timber frames both at the top and bottom. The contemporary swirly patterned carpet was way before its time and suffered the bottle green front door, but the gorgeous, moss green 60s patterned, concertina vinyl door between the lounge and the kitchen stole the show, as the girls perpetually pulled it open and shut until they were banned from ever touching it again.

The lounge had a double fire box in the form of a salmon coloured brick fireplace with a mantle of black shiny glass, carrying carefully selected ornaments, which lead to another set of three glass doors, again covered with fixed white terylene curtains. For a time, Mavis kept her ladies' cigars in a special box on the mantelpiece.

Alan's Peter Stuyvesant cigarettes were also very much a part of the home in those early days. The second firebox was meant to store wood but the family had not taken to using it for this purpose so it was converted into a small bookshelf. The lounge-room soon sported two moss green, wing back chairs and a set of triangle-shaped stacked light wood veneer side tables trimmed in a gold edging, which locked into each other by virtue of their decreasing sizes.

*Mangles Street lounge room 1961*

One of the chairs was placed near the bookshelves where Mavis mostly sat. Her prized books were kept there yielding information on beautiful works of art and the ever-increasing collection of the educational *Life* series of books that came one by one in the mail. The girls' favourite books were the photographic stills from the movies, showing movie stars from the 1920s to the 60s. But tucked discreetly in amongst all those was the odd book on the advanced philosophy of yoga and another on the yoga postures, as were the book on palmistry and another on astrology. A small bible held its own in amongst all this.

*Eleanor, Gail, Julie and Susan in the driveway ready for Church and Sunday school 1962. Alan's iconic BY 714 number plate began its life on this Holden.*

Following church and Sunday school was the delicious Sunday roast, after which Alan often took the family out for a Sunday afternoon drive. Of course, during this time he was quietly surveying who was building what, where and when. Mavis on the other hand was always looking for ideas and the girls were hanging out for the end, when the purchase of their Sunday treat came. On a Sunday evening, dinner was allowed to be eaten in the lounge room from small bread and butter plates onto which wedges of tomato and iceberg lettuce leaves sprinkled in sugar were served with leftover sliced cold roast meat.

During the Sunday evening ritual Alan would always sit on the chair near the bookcase with one leg hanging from the arm to allow Mavis leeway to nestle into the space left. The treat, a block of Cadbury chocolate, was broken up and placed into a desert bowl to be shared around. This was a warm and inclusive time for all the family and considered a special treat in more ways than one.

At first, all three bigger girls happily slept in one room, while Gail remained bedside in a cot in the main bedroom. Eventually Gail arrived in the girls' room in a big safe cot placed near the door. A safe cot is a roofed, timber-framed small child's bed, encapsulated in flywire to prevent babies absconding.

Mavis used the middle room of this three-bedroom home. Often referred to as the junk room, but in reality, it was Mavis's studio. Here she sewed and painted in oils and planned all manner of household beautifications.

The house seemed so big the girls spent hours playing 'hotels' especially after the instalment of a solid black telephone, which sat on a clever piece of furniture called a telephone table seat, in the passage that ran alongside the bedrooms. The telephone was installed so that Alan's business could continue outside office hours. Mavis and the girls received special phone answering instructions and a note pad was to be left by the phone as it was considered imperative to take down names and numbers. Try as we all did, no-one was especially good at it. A few years into the 60s the black phone made its way to a new position next to the kitchen table, as the evening business calls were increasing and dinners were being burnt.

Yet another object arrived, which changed the household forever. Two men in overalls delivered a television set. But no-one could see it until a mammoth television antenna was constructed in the back garden. The support wires stretched across the entire yard before being anchored firmly in the ground. The antenna soared high into the air between the septic tanks and the brick barbeque.

*Julie aged 8, Gail 10 months, and Eleanor aged 6, in their swim wear under the Hills hoist, in front of the brick barbeque with TV aerial wires stretched across in the background, 1961*

At first the girls believed the television was bought specifically to watch the news, but soon learnt of its many treasures, as slowly the watching hours increased beyond the news and BP Pick-a-box. The thrill of Superman, the Cisco Kid and the Mickey Mouse Club entered their lives, somehow viewed through a veil of snow or darting horizontal zigzag lines, which took the picture on a continuously rolling journey all of which distorted the sound, making for a nauseating experience. The wonder of the television set was that it could be turned to face the kitchen table on the other side of the moss green, vinyl concertina door. This was because Alan's evening homecoming, the news and dinner often collided (in a good way).

Of course, things were tight during this process and Alan worked extra hard to establish himself in the farm equipment sales world. The family saw him briefly in the mornings around 7am for breakfast which he mostly made for everyone and then sometimes well after 7pm at night. A monument began to emerge on the stove as Mavis gradually learnt to store his dinner within a layer of the new 1960s innovation of stacked steamer saucepans. The oven in the slow combustion stove tended to dry a plated meal out too much.

*Susan aged 4, in the kitchen with slow combustion stove in the background and the radio on the front counter ever ready with the news for Alan and the morning programs for Mavis. Standing guard on the right is their first electric fridge. c.1961*

# *Synchronicity*

Aside from the focus on his business and a busy home life, more and more Alan was finding his partner and boss, Bill Dixon, was not always reliable.

On a payday in 1963, Dixon was missing, making it impossible to pay his staff their due wages, and the bank would not allow Alan a withdrawal. Alan worried about how he was going to honour their staff's wages.

Added to Alan's displeasure was the appearance of his salesman, Clive Butcher, who had returned to the workshop much earlier than he should have that day. Clive rolled in at 11am and found a harassed Alan concerned about raising £700 to pay the wages of 15 employees. Clive had in fact been out in the bush, and was supposed to be still working out there, but he had already sold a Ford tractor for £750 and had decided he didn't want to carry that amount of cash around, so had dutifully returned to hand it over to Alan. (There were no mobile phones and very limited access to landlines.) The staff were duly paid their wages without ever suspecting any of the initial angst.

Sadly, the business was deteriorating and the staffs' wages were not the only bills in jeopardy, as many outstanding accounts could not be paid on time. Eventually, due to some untoward business which saw Dixon declared bankrupt in 1964, Alan offered Dixon £2,600, payable over three years including all assets and liabilities. Dixon was not in a position to argue and accepted.

Alan bought Dixon out and took over the dealership. To do this he had put everything into the business plus overdrafts from the bank. In that same year Alan registered the partnership name as 'A&M Parsons', something he and Mavis had created when the farm was acquired in 1952 (this business name was still registered in 2014).

Eventually, all Dixon had left was his car as he had left his wife for someone else. However, he soon ran into trouble again, this time asking Alan to pay him out. Alan obliged and in the end Dixon was only paid a total of £2000. Dixon then disappeared. News of him surfaced some time later revealing he had ended up in jail for stealing from his employer.

Under the new name of A&M Parsons, the 1964 dealership underwent tighter management, which enabled all debts to be paid out within ten months. By having a good team of employees, Alan says: 'My philosophy was, "the harder we work, the luckier we become."'

Alan spent extremely long hours building up the business and regaining customer trust. By so doing, the business took off and became a thriving enterprise of sales and service soon to be recognised throughout the South West of WA.

His customers often remained loyal. One such person was Greenbushes character Bluey James who, over the course of their association, purchased 26 trucks. Bluey went on to become the Mayor of Greenbushes, which then saw a continuation of his loyalty as the Shire council also took up the purchasing of trucks and other equipment.

Alan had often pondered over the difference between the dairy farmers in the South West and the wheat and sheep farmers of the Central Wheatbelt. He realised dairy farmers could plan because they were paid for their milk produce like clockwork, whereas wheat and sheep farmers faced the inconsistency of weather and market prices. Dairy farmers could confidently plan to purchase new machinery while their counterparts frequently put such decisions off or took financial risks. Being situated in the South West meant Alan too could plan. He made it his business to be aware of the needs of farmers and the like in his area, often checking that machinery was running well or letting customers know of just the right kind of equipment for their needs and price range. Alan made a point of looking after his customers with a caring eye.

## *A story of Alan's tenacity*

Jock Paul, a character who was employed as a handyman at A&M Parsons, was often seen working for Alan at all hours. This was because Jock could be called upon to accompany Alan on many of his sale delivery and trade pick-up trips, by either driving the follow up vehicle or by delivering. On one occasion in the mid-1960s, the pair

*From left: Noel Hardy (Zone Manager IHC), Jack Porter (Howard Porter), Frank Malatesta (Malatesta Transport) and Alan Parsons (A & M Parsons) at the introduction of the new model International ACCO truck, 1966*

were returning from one such mission when Alan noticed he may be able to achieve a sales record if he made a little extra effort; in Alan's words:

One day in the mid-1960s turned out to be a record of sorts in sales. I had delivered a new hay-baler to a farmer in Capel early in the morning. In the meantime, he had wrecked his hay-rake so he ordered a new one when I arrived.

*Jock Paul, the handyman on our payroll, had delivered a set of disc harrows to a farmer at Boyanup to do his firebreaks at the same time. We both arrived back at the dealership about the same time. There was a chap looking at a second-hand Bedford truck at the time, so I sold it to him.*

*Then came a phone call from a farmer at Dardanup enquiring as to if we had a second-hand baler. We did, so I sold it to him and Jock went out to deliver it. Whilst on a roll that day the business sold two new hay mowers as well. I then took an order for a new six-wheeler tip truck, but as the tip body had to be built, delivery took place about two weeks later.*

*I had sold a second-hand Austin truck a couple of days earlier, which had to be modified and serviced and delivered to the buyer in Donnybrook that night, as the truck was booked to take a load to Perth early the next morning.*

*I drove it to Donnybrook. Jock followed in the car to bring me home. By the time I finished the paperwork, including hire purchase documents and then a beer with the customer, it was about 10.30 pm.*

*As we drove home, I was adding up the day's activities and thought, 'what a day, what else can we do?' It was then I remembered a young farmer at Wellington Mills who had been in talking about a new tractor. I instructed Jock to drive to this chap's property. We found it around 11.30 pm, knocked on his door, woke him up and as he was not connected to electricity, he came out holding a kerosene lamp. I immediately told him why we were there and it was to be his decision alone if he wished to place an order for the new tractor.*

*He signed the order at 11.55 pm, completing my day.*

Jock Paul was a loyal, hard-working Scotsman, who gave Alan and the fledgling business his allegiance for many years. However, Jock struggled with an alcohol problem. Alan explains a situation, which had to be addressed:

*I drove in from Perth about 8pm on the Friday before New Year. As my headlights swept the front of the showroom, two chaps were fighting in the driveway. It was Max McCamish and Jock Paul. Max was a traffic inspector and Jock was on our payroll. For many years, I used the Bunbury traffic officers to drive new trucks home from Perth. As they had weekend rosters, they had two days off mid-week, so there were always drivers available. They were reliable and responsible guys and they enjoyed the extra income.*

*That day, I had suggested to Ernie Davies, the Service Manager, that he get some drinks in at knock-off time for the workshop fellows to celebrate the coming New Year. Somehow, Max had an invite. He was in uniform and had arrived on his police motorbike. I do not know what caused the fight, but they were dinkum, blood and torn clothes showing. I pulled them apart and ordered them both to get in my car. They both lived in Carey Park and as I drove them home, I told Jock he was fired forthwith and Max was told he would never be called to drive again.*

*They both walked to the Dealership next morning, Max for his motorbike and to apologise, Jock for his car and ready for work. I had to tell him the office lady would make up his pay and his job was finished.*

*I met his wife a few weeks later and she thanked me profusely. Jock had always been a heavy drinker but had never been fired before. She told me he had not had a drink since that night, and as far as I know, he never drank again.*

*It is not always easy being the boss.*

## The re-emergence of Uncle Keith

When Alan set up in Bunbury, Keith Muir, his uncle, began to cart used oil from many different locations around the town. It had become illegal to tip old oil onto the ground. At first, he collected old oil from garages and the like and took it to be cleaned and recycled elsewhere; however, never to miss an opportunity, he soon began refining the oil himself. As business became more lucrative, this led to Alan

Uncle Keith, 1960s

selling Keith a couple of Mitsubishi trucks. Darryl, his son, was not the same to deal with and although Darryl eventually took over the business, a working relationship with Alan could not be nurtured.

[Darryl married Meryl and had three children, one of whom is Kelly. Curiously in the late 1970s Kelly met Gail (Alan's youngest daughter) socially, and the two of developed a close friendship - even travelling overseas together.]

## *Meanwhile back on the job and it's showtime*

The Brunswick Show was, and still is, a major South West highlight in the agricultural world. There has always been a huge turnout of businesses keen to show off their wares and services, and in the late 1960s Alan was in the thick of it. Mavis wanted to spend time with her seriously ill mother, Annie, who was in Intensive Care at the Bunbury Regional Hospital, so Alan took Susan and Gail with him to the Show. As events unfolded it was to be at this particular Show that Alan had his last cigarette.

Attending the Brunswick Show is an annual 'must do' for the farming community. The showground event is one of Australia's biggest one-day shows, according to the Brunswick Agriculture Show archives. The trade and machinery displays showcase what is on offer in the South West. The ring events are always embraced with enthusiasm and are a pleasure to watch. In the 1960s, log chopping was held on a large 1.5 metre high, purpose-built stand allowing the crowds much better views of the exciting event.

On this occasion, the log chopping had finished and the Grand Parade was just starting. Alan's farm equipment display stand happened to be between the log chopping stand and the show ring, so when the ring events began and people moved towards the seating around the central showground Alan could not see, but by the time the Grand parade had started six or seven guys had climbed onto the log chopping stand to watch.

As no-one was looking at Alan's stand, he thought it would be a good idea to join the guys (most of whom he knew) on the log chopping stand. From there he could both watch his display and Grand Parade. He was on the log chopping stand for about 10 minutes when the whole thing collapsed. Alan says: "I woke up in the ambulance halfway to Bunbury."

The look on Mavis's face must have been incomprehensible when they wheeled her husband into Intensive Care and set him up in the bed right next to her mother's. It was fortunate that Mavis was already at the hospital, sitting with her very unwell mother when they brought Alan for observation. Alan says: "I must have had a cigarette at the time of the collapse because I have never smoked since."

Fortunately, Gail and Sue had been gathered up by family friends, who kept them in their care, but not before some woman had told Susan their father was dead. In shock and attempting to hide this devastating news from eight-year-old Gail, Sue tried to keep it to herself. They were then told he was alive and a quietly hysterical Susan had to be taken to the St Johns tent at the showground to be reassured he really was alive, although unconscious and a little damaged. But Gail, now confused and isolated from events, says she only knew something untoward was happening when someone else took them home. Gail said: "I later found a bag in the kitchen of dad's bloodied clothes. I then went outside and cried." Eventually Mavis, also shocked, explained what had happened. Gail said: "Took mum ages to tell me, but as a child 'ages' feels like forever."

Some of the other men suffered injuries but only one suffered permanent damage (to his ankle). However, absolutely no-one considered claiming insurance. It simply just was not done in those days. Having been cleared Alan was sent home the next day, and naturally returned to work the following day. But there was something different. Alan, true to his word, has not had a cigarette since.

# The horse incident

Another challenging episode, which also threatened to stop the 'unstoppable Alan' in his tracks, occurred around the same time. The horse incident as told by Alan:

*Ernie Pilatti, a friend and customer, had rung on a Sunday night wanting truck parts urgently. As he had to drive from Buckingham (the other side of Collie), I offered to collect the parts and meet him at Roelands. At Waterloo, a misty rain had started, the wipers were pretty ordinary, and a car coming towards me put his lights on high beam, blinding me. I had slowed but as soon as I passed him there was a horse right in front of me. I hit the animal in the back legs and it came back over the car. By the time I pulled up the horse was laying in water beside the road, screaming in pain. The offending car had driven off (never found out who it was. I guess his theory of lights on high beam, was to warn me). I knew the property and the farmer who owned the horse so I walked to his house. He was not at all cooperative (assuming he was in the wrong because the horse was on the road not in the paddock), so I used his phone to ring the police who also did not want to know as there was no one hurt.*
*I eventually rang a vet who came and shot the horse. I rang one of our employees to come and take me to finish the delivery, then home. I got a tow truck to collect the car. Ernie got his parts.*
*I bought a new car the next morning ... and carried on.*

And carry on he did. Alan started winning awards for sales, and recognition of his work with International and the like, which took him and Mavis on their first interstate trip to Melbourne, followed by a trip to Fiji. In 1972, they went to the USA: Chicago, LA, and Fort Wayne where an International Harvester factory was located. These early trips included several more visits to the eastern states (but there was more travel to come in the 1980s, courtesy of other merchandise franchises Alan worked with during his re-emergence: more about that later).

Many sales records were broken in the 33 years of trading as A & M Parsons, including the sale of around 3,500 new and used trucks, and record sales of farm machinery. To achieve this, on average, Alan kept a strong team on the payroll of about 15 people.

## Mavis at 101 Mangles Street

As the girls grew so did the need to divide them into twos and appoint them new sleeping arrangements. Pretty wall papers were chosen and painting occurred in soft pastels. A little, old, green Austin car, with small orange arms that flew out from the side panel between the doors to indicate a left or right turn, was purchased and parked in the new two-car brick garage. The little green Austin would ferry the girls to swimming lessons in the bay at the Jetty Baths during the summer and then to the outskirts of town for a milkshake or a spider. As the school year started, the girls were taken to the Convent of Mercy for music and elocution lessons during the term. The little green Austin, whom Mavis called Betty, or Elizabeth during contentious moments, would only go into town around the Back Beach; granted this was the long way but without the menace of traffic according to Mavis, and would only be parked opposite the convent, a practice she was to follow all her driving life no matter where she lived in Bunbury.

This woman grew wings of her own after marching the girls off to Mrs King's ballet classes on Saturday afternoons. Alice King spotted Mavis's talents a mile off and soon had Mavis playing the piano for some of the dance practice, but no-one could replace Mrs Williams, Alice's ever-faithful pianist. Then came the ballet concert and together, Alice King and Mavis developed a keen sense of what costumes were required.

Once it was learned that Mavis could not only draw and sew but could also sing, Alice lured her into some of her Musical Comedy shows, but the little green Austin did not venture out in the evenings; Mavis was always picked up by a fellow thespian. Before long, Mavis was up till the wee small hours bending over the kitchen table

*From top left; Eleanor, Julie, Gail and Susan in their ballet costumes all made by Mavis*

that was covered in costume designs, all neatly rendered to enable their recreation.

The house became embroiled in yards of gorgeous fabrics, glitter, beads, pom-poms and mammoth amounts of tulle out of which four tutus emerged. How a man of Alan's standing emerged every day from this chaos of feminine pursuits into his world of trucks and sweaty men is one of those delightful puzzles.

By the late '60s, both Eleanor and Julie were at Kobeelya, a small boarding school in Katanning for girls and their horses. Although neither girl had a horse, both still had the 'country' in their bones. At around the same time, Alan's father fell into dire financial difficulties so Alan simply doubled his efforts to ensure both that his father was rescued and his girls remained unaffected. With so much hard work, letting off steam was always welcomed.

Alan and Mavis in early 1970s

## Friendships in the '60s and '70s

Soon Alan began to make new friends and although, according to Mavis, many had their own problems, Alan always enjoyed the company of his mates. The names of these guys linger. The 1960s brought Pop Ganger, Phil Tucket, Jock Paul, Noel Hardy and Neville Perryman, just to name a few. Ross Manolas arrived on the scene in the 1960s. Alan, who has always believed in the personal approach, was in the habit of knocking on farmer's doors to introduce himself and offer his farm machinery services. Alan believed that unless you were able to get your feet under the kitchen table of a potential buyer, you did not stand a hope of getting a sale.

Ross had a farm at Kirup (followed by properties in Ferguson and Picton). It was at his Kirup property that the two met. It turned out Ross Manolas and Rodney Johnston (Alan's first friend in Bunbury) were mates and eventually they would gather Alan up on a Friday evening for drinks at the South West Club. This led to involvement in the Bunbury Rotary Club, which Alan joined in 1972. Between the three of them the urge to support one another was at its best on Friday evenings. It developed into a Friday night of laughs, a 'Play Night' tradition that lasted many years. The ever observant and amused Mavis wrote an adaption of a popular rhyme and it was handed in at a Rotary meeting, which of course ensured they all got fined:

*Rub a dub dub*
*Three men in the pub*
*and who do you think they be?*
*Alan and Ross*
*and Rodney's the boss*
*on their way home from Rotary.*

## *Beginning community service*

Alan joined the St Johns Ambulance Committee in the late 1960s and thus began a lifelong commitment to community service, although not without some pleasure as mentioned. However, according Alan, this particular committee was a little different:

*The committee consisted of about six or seven well intentioned elderly ladies, who brought their knitting to the meetings. The previous president set this up to suit himself, it lasted about 18 months. Within four years St Johns had secured four new ambulances.*

After his contribution to St Johns, Alan attended a meeting on 22 June 1977, convened following a previous discussion at Parliament House. The meeting brought together eight state farm machinery dealerships with the intention of forming an association. Duly achieved, it expanded to a national association. The following is taken from an article in the Farmer's Weekly, 31st June 1977:

*TAXATION, fuel costs, parts supplies and transport regulations were among the key issues discussed at the inaugural Farm Machinery Dealers Association (FMDA) meeting at El Caballo Blanco, Wooroloo, on June 22nd, 1977.*

The inaugural committee comprised Alan Parsons and Tim Ratten, Esperance (southern zone); Max Carson and Greg Humphries, Corrigin (central zone); John Jolly, Dalwallinu; and Graham Bunny, Dalwallinu (northern zone). It seems Alan became disappointed with the underachieving outcome, saying:

*The WA Association of Farm Machinery Dealers was all brands of machinery and all dealers who were interested. It did not achieve what I thought could have happened.*

However, the Hon. MLA Sandy Lewis was very pleased with most of the issues tackled by the Association, including sales tax, tariffs, credit laws, occupational health and safety, towing of farm machinery and warranties.

As mentioned, Alan joined Rotary in 1972, staying involved for some 42 years. He was elected president of Rotary from 1982-83, although before that could be realised, Rotary had a specific agenda that had to be followed before the 'change-over' could be affected from one president to another. In 1982 the incoming Rotary president had to have a worthy project, which would benefit the community and for which a president had to lead the way in fundraising for his project.

Alan was always alert to innovations and was interested in a new invention used to extract people from the entangled mess of metal cars following nasty car crashes. The new-fangled device was nicknamed the 'Jaws of Life'. Wanting to give something of great value to a worthy beneficiary became a challenge when Alan tried to find a home for the extraordinary lifesaving tool. Alan says:

*I first thought that because the ambulance would be in attendance at an accident that they would be very appreciative of something that saved lives, but they were unable to manage the Jaws of Life because it was a cutting device for vehicles not people and neither would it fit into the already tightly fitted out ambulance.*

*Next, I tried the Bunbury Police, again they also were not interested because of all the equipment they were required to carry. And as an air-cooled engine was necessary to drive the 'Jaws of Life' their vehicles also lacked the space.*

*It is important to understand that during those days these institutions were able to make their own decisions.*

*Finally, I went to the Bunbury Fire Brigade and it turned out to be a perfect fit for their purposes. In fact, not long after Rotary's $700 Jaws for Life presentation to the Bunbury Brigade, it was duly noted that, in time, the State Fire Department had also adopted the Jaws of Life in order to cut into car bodies and the like to release trapped victims. A good outcome for all I think.*

Whilst in Rotary Alan won the Paul Harris Fellowship Award in 1989, one of the highest honours Rotary can bestow upon a person. Recipients are Rotarians and community professionals all over the world. Alan humbly says of the honour that he felt it was offered to him because Rotary had to find someone to present the award to, and as he had achieved a few things, he was it. Instead Alan felt very strongly that Rotary needed to look further afield and deeper into the community itself for worthwhile recipients. As usual Alan's follow through saw two community members receive their well-earned awards:

*I got more enjoyment nominating Bishop Hawkins and Sister Romanus for the award. They both had done more for Bunbury and its people than the whole of Rotary Bunbury Club had done. I got a bit of opposition because of the religious aspect but they were duly awarded their Paul Harris Fellowships. A proud day for all.*

A&M Parsons International Harvester Dealership entrance off Forrest Avenue, Bunbury. The second-hand trucks in the yard were trade-ins. Business was booming c.1968

# CHAPTER EIGHT

## "We need a Parsons-proof fence"
### Barry McCormack

### Business as usual in the 1960s & 70s

All this time the potential of the South West was building and the need for trucks was growing. Alan developed relationships with 11 shire councils, all of whom needed trucks and machinery. Barry McCormack, a former zone manager who took up a dealership in farm machinery at Kulin had said at the time, 'We need a Parsons-proof fence'. He wanted Alan to stay out of his territory so that he would have half a chance.

Trucks were also needed for spot sawmills and stock transport; the farm machinery industry was entering its heyday. After WWII and the post-war struggles of the 1940s and 1950s, farmers had minimal farm machinery and there was little money for improvements. However, the 1960s saw a growth spurt in the economy and rural production; farmers had money to purchase a new tractor and the latest hay cutting and hay baling equipment.

The rural boom, from 1949 to 1969, affected the growth because during this time land clearing on farms almost doubled. A feature article titled *The History of*

*Machinery* in Elders Weekly 70th Anniversary edition notes: 'Sheep numbers trebled, and wheat acreage and production increased nearly three times'. Tractor production had to increase at the same rate. But because of the sheer size of cropping and the demand for faster operations, farm machinery had to change with the times, and change it did. Everything had to get bigger and more versatile. Automation and electronic technology was on the rise.

The need for buses also grew because school buses were only allowed to operate for 15 years. Together with Howard Porter, Alan developed buses that fitted onto the International chassis. As these buses became a necessity for the regulated school bus service in all surrounding Shires in the region and the Perth metropolitan area, the exercise developed into a profitable venture.

It is interesting to note that in the 1930s, Alan's Uncle Bert had previously and ingeniously converted a truck chassis into the bus he used to transport the Collie miners. Bert also converted the bus back again and later sold the 'cross-dressing' truck to Alan's father.

Meanwhile, following a similar principle Alan hit upon the notion of a conversion for the International van. In this instance, he created ambulances. This all came about when Alan met Barney Hay, who was the Mayor and Bailiff of Bunbury, as well as the President of the Bunbury Ambulance Association. Barney was a visionary. His work in real estate saw him move house some 23 times, as he predicted the areas that were about to move ahead (even his chooks were so well practised that when a box was put in their pen they simply got in).

Alan was approached to get a price for an ambulance to be fitted out and set onto an International chassis. Pre-delivery of the ambulance was difficult because Hay had yet to inform the committee. Nonetheless, once they had delivery of the first one they went onto buy another four. Other Shires also began to purchase new ambulances from Alan thus seeing the South West well serviced with outstanding new vehicles that were suited to emergency response calls.

All up Alan sold 20 ambulances to all the South West towns, replacing the troublesome old Dodge ambulances. Again, synchronicity played a role because International could produce a van which was highly suitable for conversion to ambulances. But it was Alan's imagination and perspicacity that brought it about.

The ambulances took two to three months to fit out into the International van body. The Bunbury Ambulance Committee, led by Barney Hay, took a risk in moving from the classic Dodge van into the International van, but from then on the stage was set and Alan was able to secure further sales throughout the South West.

The old, obsolete Dodge ambulances often ended their days in the hands of local 'surfies'. The old Bedford and Austin buses were turned into motor homes, or buses for transport for local community nursing homes and schools etc. At one stage, Alan worried that he had a yard full of buses not trucks; in this regard Alan took chances selling the second-hand buses to individuals and groups for community and other creative uses.

Alan made it a practice to remember all his clients' phone numbers and number plates. It is hard to conceive how many hours Alan spent driving from farm to farm, maintaining that people responded best to his personal approach. His belief in the value of cold canvassing meant he would also call on people he didn't know.

International Harvester used to put on sales campaigns once or twice a year when their sales were down. They would establish a target and whoever reached the sales target won a trip. One year the sales target was set on tractors. Alan decided to drive a tractor directly onto the farms, using an old second-hand Austin truck to transport the said tractor to a remote locality.

When out on the old Balingup road where he knew no one, he drove onto a farm and got to the sheds just as the dairy farmer was finishing milking. The farmer had an old Fordson tractor in his shed. Alan explained what he was doing and the farmer invited him to join him over breakfast in the house. Alan sat down with the farmer and by about 10.30 he was unloading the tractor and soon had it hooked onto some disc ploughs.

But the farmer still wasn't sure it was what he needed. Then it was lunch time and Alan was invited to stay for lunch. By about 4.00 pm Alan was loading the farmer's old Fordson tractor onto the truck with all the paperwork signed up. The next day he arrived back in the same place, with another new tractor on the back of his truck, and repeated the exercise with the neighbouring farmer across the road, again achieving the desired result. Alan's philosophy of 'you can't sell a farmer anything until you get your feet under their kitchen table' was well employed that week.

At around the same time the International Harvester national sales manager for farm machinery happened to be in Bunbury. This person was a Canadian who had never been to Western Australia. In order to observe Alan's sales campaign and technique he booked into a hotel planning to stay a number of nights. Alan arranged it so that the next day it was the national sales manager who drove the tractor from farm to farm, while he followed along behind. All was going well when all of a sudden, the heavens opened and rain bucketed down. Alan wound his window up and kept following the poor bloke who had no protection from the elements and was completely soaked — Alan reckoned there was no point in them both getting wet. In spite of this experience, the sales manager wouldn't have missed the hands-on action for the world.

## Changes in the farm machinery industry

During Sir Charles Court's premiership of WA in the 1970s, as mentioned previously, a group of farm machinery dealers, representing all makes and brands of farm machinery, met together with the purpose of forming an Association. The idea was that an Association of this kind would advise the manufacturers, defining rural Western Australia into agricultural, produce and meat growing zones.

They met at Parliament House because the dealer, Sandy Lewis, was also a politician. Different farming applications were occurring around the South West; farm machinery businesses had to develop quickly to keep up with grain, sheep, produce and dairy farmers, which created a new complexity for the dealerships. The group came together to solve this problem. They divided WA into zones, thereby framing areas which required specific farming equipment. The dealers could then sort themselves into supplying specific equipment for the specific farming requirements of each zone. Sir Charles Court would sit with them, contributing some valuable and considered advice, and then return to his Premier's duties leaving the dealers to their meeting.

Bridgetown was an exceptionally good area for Alan and as he was acquainted with a good number of people there, he always liked to exhibit any new trucks and tractors at the Bridgetown Show. On this particular occasion Sir Charles Court had lost the election and Brian Burke was in power. Nothing much was happening so Alan went to look at the side shows. He saw a cap with a motto written across it: 'I am their leader. Which way did they go'. Alan bought the cap and as he walked around the corner, he bumped into Sandy Lewis and Charlie Court. They asked what was in his paper bag and Alan revealed the cap, adding he had just bought it for Brian Burke. Alan reckons Charlie Court laughed well into next week.

## *Collaboration and the Pilbara*

In the early 1960s, Lang Hancock found iron ore in the Pilbara region of Western Australia and opened it up to mining. It was tough 'up North': the roads weren't sealed and many were not much more than tracks. This was never understood by the WA southerners until South West truckies ventured into trucking up North, hoping to make their fortune.

Frank Malatesta, who ran a local South West truck company, found out the hard way when he decided he would send half-a-dozen trucks up with semi-trailers, loaders and all the necessary gear. His mistake? He had put recapped tyres on the heavy vehicles, and the rough roads did the rest, ripping the tyres to shreds. Sadly, Malatesta (which means bad head in Italian) lost his contract when his trucks failed to arrive at their destination. Although he had made all possible preparations for the trip, he learnt a difficult lesson about tyres on unsealed roads.

A&M Parsons, on the other hand, quietly did well with the North West venture, with eighteen International trucks sold, one by one, in the most unexpected manner. After a discreet phone call from the local Ford car dealer and financier Norman Dorsett, it was agreed Norm would initiate the unusual practice of referring buyers to Alan. Dorsett considered Ford trucks inappropriate for such work but saw the International trucks as a superior machine, worthy of consideration for the job. He also wanted to keep his customers happy, so began to redirect his clients. As more people wanted to follow work in the North West, more trucks were needed — as was the finance to purchase one. The buyers would appear at Alan's office door carrying a sealed envelope from Dorsett. The first sealed envelope brought into Alan at his dealership discreetly suggested Alan include Norm's percentage in the cost. Alan did and sent the client back with all the appropriate paperwork for the purpose of obtaining finance through Norman Dorsett.

Every deal was different: sometimes a trade-in, sometimes it depended on what model was required, and what discounts were available from International at the time. Turntables, bull bars, radiators and other extras made a difference to the deal. Norman never applied pressure to Alan, allowing the whole mutual agreement to continue for its natural duration over a two-year period.

There is an early story of one particular fellow who had driven out to a sheep station to transport a load of wool back to port. The truck was a 1928 International. On the trip back, a big end bearing burnt out. He was hundreds of miles from help so shot a kangaroo to live off and proceeded to dismantle the failed bearing. He cut the leather tongue from his boot, which he soaked in the sump oil for two days, then cut it to the size of the failed bearing, fitted it, and continued his trip to port, arriving safely. This repair could never be made in the truck engines of today.

## *Cyclone Alby*

On the 4th of April 1978, an ill wind blew into town. With cyclonic wind gusts in the early evening the power was out and the transistor radio was on at the Parsons' home in Mangles Street. Unable to see clearly in the dark, Alan had inadvertently made Mavis a couple of extra strong brandy and dry drinks. The call out came over the radio to anyone with a truck who was willing to help rescue stranded people living opposite the inlet, where flood waters were pouring in. The water was already waist deep with reports of dead chickens and cats floating past. All the while hurricane-force winds were causing massive damage in the South West, with a number of buildings losing their roofs. Due to large swells, the seawater had breached the sea wall, inundating a hundred homes and 130 residents had already been evacuated when the radio announcer began calling for help.

Alan lost no time in springing into action. Julie, then 25 and visiting her parents, went with him to ride as shotgun, while Mavis, a little tipsy, went straight to bed. They first drove the car through the horrendous winds and airborne debris to the workshop where Alan knew he had the perfect truck. Getting into the workshop was another matter. Julie was told to stay in the car and watch, and if anything happened she was to act; for the duration, she was intensely fearful as she watched her father ducking and weaving through flying debris, most of which was corrugated iron sheeting from surrounding industrial shed roofs. Opening the workshop doors against these fiercely powerful forces was another feat. Alan located the truck and exited the workshop, while Julie drove the car into the workshop then quickly climbed into the waiting truck's cab, Alan meanwhile struggling against the elements again to shut the big sliding, corrugated doors.

*The 1978 cyclone gutted Julie's newly renovated farmhouse*

Making their way to East Bunbury and into the seawater that threatened to submerge more homes, they picked up as many people and pets as they could and relayed them back to a surprised Mavis and daughter Gail, tucked up in their beds at Mangles Street. Alan says there were about 30 people altogether, along with their pets and even a parrot in a cage. Julie's diaries also tell of a rogue tip-truck relentlessly searching the low-lying streets for possible rescues, their first rescuees still ensconced in the tip tray. These poor people were soaked to the bone with the unceasing, torrential rains and were standing in an ever-increasing pool of water. They were screaming to be rescued from the tip truck and its mad driver, the tops of their heads and cold fingers, just visible, gripping the edge as they scrambled up the sides to call for help. How they got in there defies the imagination. Alan caught up with the driver to alert him to his troubled passengers, but this guy was too far gone with the excitement of the rescue to see sense, insisting he was going to do another round. By then, others joined in to prevent him, and Alan returned to his own charge, deciding it was time to call it quits and head home.

Once home and with the power outage still on, he tried to pour and serve drinks to his unplanned guests, again guessing at quantities in the dark. Mavis had rounded up tea and biscuits but these people needed something more. Once the winds abated and phone calls had been made, some of their friends and relatives turned up to retrieve loved ones, but all the beds were full that night with pets everywhere.

In an interview with Beth Ferguson for the Dec 2014 issue of *The Bunbury Chamber of Commerce, Business Focus*, Alan recalled the story of the cyclone and the second-hand truck particularly well, including the fate of the truck, which Ferguson recorded in Alan's words:

*The truck had been through salt water so it would have had to have been thoroughly washed and serviced. I brought it back and wrecked it because by the late '70s we also had a wrecking yard.*

# *Christmas time with A&M Parsons*

The workshop, as Alan called it, housed numerous Father Christmas experiences for the children of staff and friends. Down would come the calendars of skimpily-clad ladies and in would go the excited but restrained children. The workshop was opened right up so that Father Christmas, who was towed in on a trailer hitched to the back of a tractor, could make good his escape. Children's names were called as little gifts, pulled from the sack, turned bewildered faces into smiling ones. The blokes had beers while the ladies took afternoon tea and the children consumed small bottles of either Kola, Fanta, or Lemonade.

*Father Christmas and Alan with Neville Perryman in the background*

The Christmas staff party hosted by Alan and Mavis was the company's biggest social event — or perhaps better described as Mavis's biggest social challenge. Out would come the platters decked in miniature red onions and pineapple pieces, skewered by toothpicks on cubes of cheddar, and stuck neatly around an orange placed in a curved indentation in the centre of the platter. There would be prunes wrapped in bacon, also pierced by toothpicks, cheese darlings, puffed pastry creations and curried eggs. Wooden bowls of potato chips and barbeque shapes would be deposited about, and the mysterious mock chicken sandwiches were offered to those who dared. The backyard took on a new persona with the lawn mown, night lighting and red cloths strewn across trestle tables upon which paper plates were arranged around platters. The men would stand about, either around the kegs of beer or the aproned cook at the barbeque, while the reticent children sipped on pineapple juice mixed with lemonade, and the ladies sat on chairs in a semi-circle enjoying a sherry, a shandy or perhaps a portagaff.

## *Selling A&M Parsons*

By the time Alan had turned 50, the farm machinery landscape was again changing. From about 1978, or possibly earlier, and unbeknown to most, the International Harvester Company was moving towards global bankruptcy. This major event collided with Alan's own realisations. Of this period Alan says:

> *I was running out of puff. I felt the market was changing here and that IH were not keeping up with the changing demands, particularly with the truck market.*

Thoughts of selling the business found their way into his daily activities. He realised he had made himself indispensable, and as the main driver of his business operations, he felt strongly it would fail if he was not at the helm. Nevertheless, things began to happen regardless. As Alan explains:

> *I cannot remember how it started, but I got a call from a chap in Melbourne, who said they had heard it was maybe for sale. I went to Melbourne, met with two guys, Charles McKinnon and Richard Hoile, who were employed by David Nicholas who had inherited the Aspro empire.*

*They vaguely said they were interested in a motor dealership in WA but not in the city. They needed a base in WA to approach and acquire two public companies in Perth, namely Sydney Atkinson, the big General Motors dealer in Perth and Winterbottoms, the next biggest car dealer.*

*It all sounded vague but interesting so I accepted that their auditors come and check our figures. This took about a month and the two above-named chaps spent time in Bunbury, learning how to run a truck dealership.*

*A walk in, walk out, figure was struck and duly paid. I was offered six months as an advisor and general help on a fat salary. That lasted about one month and I could see they had no idea of the industry so I resigned. They had leased the premises for five years.*

*I then joined Steere and Clarke as a salesman, selling farms etc. Rodney Johnston had set this up, hoping I would buy the business, so he and Les Clarke could retire.*

Johnston may have instigated a great idea but even though he led Alan to water, he could not make him drink. Instead Alan had a look around, during a break from work, before it became apparent his modus operandi was entirely different to Johnston's; he thrived on a different kind of challenge.

## *The earth-moving business: Alan and the Jimmy Hull story*

Meanwhile, another enterprise had been hatching in Waroona since the 1950s, which soon began to interface with A&M's business profile. The Waroona business was started by Jimmy Hull, who had a shortened leg and wore a big, built-up boot to compensate. His father, not unlike Alan's, had told him he would never amount to anything because of his physical handicap, although Alan's speech impediment was in no way holding him back now. Jimmy Hull, likewise, was headed for big things. He had begun his contractor business with one small bulldozer and by the time Alan met him he ran a sizable concern. Alan says;

*When I met Jimmy in the early sixties he must have had 30 bulldozers and about 40 trucks, backhoes and all the gear it takes to run an earthmoving show. From the late sixties, I began to sell him trucks and we became social friends from then on.*

Around this time Alan was negotiating with Esanda Finance to provide clients with funds to purchase the trucks he intended to sell to Jim Hull. In the course of his dealings he began a business association with the manager of ESA Bank, Neville Perryman, who had been transferred to Bunbury around 1963/4. Alan, an Esanda dealer, introduced Neville to Jim because Esanda, the commercial/financial component of the ESA Bank (soon to become the ANZ Bank in 1969) was likely to be able to assist Jim's clientele.

Alan had used the Esanda Finance for his clients to enable the purchase his product. Leasing or hire purchase was the two avenues available to them although many customers supplied their own avenue of finance. Alan says of Perryman:

*Perryman had not experienced the Esanda arm, so he initially made himself available to travel with me on deals so he could learn the system. He soon became a popular banker in the area of transport and farming.*
*I used Esanda hire purchase or leasing for clients who needed finance to purchase trucks etc. We never had a deal go bad in the 33 years of business.*
*Perryman's wife Betty was the daughter of Spanney's in Corrigin for whom Mavis worked when she and I met, so that is how we all became friends, especially Neville and myself.*

Alan and Neville Perryman forged a strong friendship, which extended into many leisure activities between the families. However, a curious number of events took place which eventually changed everything:

*In 1978, on our way to the airport to fly to the UK with the Johnstons, I called on Jimmy Hull as he had won a big contract and needed some new gear. I signed him up for eight new eight-wheeler tip trucks. International Harvester told me it was one of the biggest regional orders they had ever received. Howard Porter supplied and fitted the hoist gear as the trucks arrived from Melbourne* and Jim's workshop built and fitted the tip bodies. The last one was delivered to Jim the week we got back from our trip.

By 1982 his health was failing him and he was losing control of the day to day running of the business. He had also won the contract to do all the earthworks required to build the railway line from Collie to Worsley, which had just opened up.

At that point, I had sold my dealership and was selling the odd farm for Steere and Clarke. Jim offered me a job managing and controlling the railway job. He was desperate for the right people. I declined, not wishing to go under that sort of pressure. Jim died of a heart attack some months later.

Jim's sons were too young to take control. The office manager had a pretty good idea of the mess and the rorts that were happening, so between him and Jim's wife Joan, they asked me to oversee the day-to-day running of it all until it was all sorted.

With over 100 employees and 96 utes for them to get to work, plus all the other dramas, it was huge and a challenge I was not sure I could handle. I had to visit three or four teams of workers in the initial stage and tell them that their jobs were secure at that point. The vibes told me, 'who is this guy that came in to tell us what to do.' At least 20 of them thought they should have been offered the job. A bit of a learning curve for me.

However, between Bob Shannon, the office manager, and myself after some months, we had the control sorted, then we started the mammoth job of valuing every thing.

At one point, I went to Melbourne and left instructions for the manager of all vehicles, to find ALL the utes, put a name to them and list who was using them, and then set up a system of the driver signing for each fill of petrol, and register kilometres travelled each day. As a colossal amount of petrol was being 'softened' each night, to wives' cars etc., this made me unpopular but some sort of control was taking place. Several of the workforce had to be fired as more thieving was found.

In the middle of all this, Neville Perryman, who had been transferred to the Perth office, with a drop in salary and responsibility, applied for the job of *manager that I had set up. He applied pressure on Joan and I had the sad job of telling him to go away, and advising Joan to tell him likewise. There ended 12 years of friendship. At that point, receivers had been appointed, the business was being sold to John Court, whom I would not recommend and the rest is history.*

'The rest is history' saw Charles, Jim's brother, who originally had a shed out the back of Waroona for second-hand gear, move into Jim's custom-built premises. Charles Hull fell on his feet and created the contracting empire Jimmy dreamt of. Alan explains:

*When Jim built his huge workshop and office complex on the South Western Highway it was finished but not officially opened when he invited Mavis and myself to lunch with them on a Sunday. He put me in his Mercedes and drove to the site. He drove right inside and around the workshop. He would not get out of the car but sat there and said, 'this will be my Memorial'. I have always remembered that day. He died about two years later.*

*At that point Joan, Jimmy's wife, did not step in to run the business but she did become friends with the section managers, giving her a bit of an idea what was happening. Jimmy's immediate family were too young to take on the immense responsibility. The business needed leadership and Alan, having a huge respect for Jim Hull, was pleased to be able to tidy it up for the future and the subsequent sale of the whole operation.*

*Charles (Hull) was always in the background and when the Perryman incident occurred, he made his move. By then, Alan had finished his contribution, and it had become an estate matter in Jim's will.*

Charles moved, although it is not clear how or what happened. He ended up with the business premises and possibly anything that went with it, including John Court who got gobbled up in it all somehow. If you drive down the Southwest Highway, you will see signage in huge lettering, defining his claim: 'Charles Hull Contracting'.

Further to the story of Alan's mate Jimmy Hull, Alan tells of the outcome for Jimmy's wife, Joan:

*The other thing I have thought of, Jim had a big job going on in Mandurah for a property developer named Robinson. Jim was owed a huge amount of money for work done and I was led to that problem. However, it became an estate matter and I was able to walk away from it. A year or two later, Joan Hull married the developer's brother, Bill Robinson, who also died about three years later.*

Trouble shooting this tricky situation seemed to fill a void for Alan when he had sold A&M Parsons and was trying to make a go of things in the farming real estate business. Alan says:

*I think I was bored with Steere and Clarke. I also think Rodney was hoping I might buy the business and he could retire.*

Neville Perryman, Alan Parsons and Rodney Johnston 1980

Although Alan, regrettably, had lost two sustaining and valued friendships during this period, throughout his subsequent soul searching, which included the farming real estate business and the Hull management experience, he began to turn back towards what he knew best with a renewed confidence.

*Alan enjoying a good laugh with Mavis*

## CHAPTER NINE

# *"You gotta get a good half-hour laugh a day"*
## *Alan Parsons*

### *A fishy tale - all things recreational*

Upon their arrival in Bunbury, Alan tried his hand at fishing by taking the girls to learn to fish off, or rather under, the old wharf. The catch of the day was always a 'blowie' but apparently the real reason no-one could catch proper fish was because they needed a boat. And it wasn't long before one manifested itself.

### *Alan's launch into the boating world*

First came a little Rickets Blue boat known for its horror trips up the Collie River. Mavis says she spent many hours waiting on the bank with a babe-in-arms and three small children at foot, while watching Alan drift off up the river as he worked to start the stalled engine.

Next came a boat which took in so much water it was almost impossible to winch it out of the river onto the boat trailer. On the shores of Koombana Bay, Mavis again saw the same view of Alan, but this time disappearing out to sea. Now surrounded by children who could swim she commanded Julie, her eldest, into the water to swim to the boat and bring Alan back to shore.

Then, came Alan's first speedboat along with Noel Hardy, the new zone manager for International for the South West. Noel, originally from South Australia, also came with a set of water skis and a family. Everyone except Mavis learnt to ski behind Cooinda. This reliable boat also introduced the family to crabbing in the Estuary.

Boating on Cooinda II on the Leschenault Estuary. Eleanor, Alan, Susan and Julie behind

Finally, came Cooinda II, a luxury craft in comparison to all that had gone before. It went on ocean trips to Rottnest Island. At this point in time Julie had her driver's licence, and what was going to be a simple, family drive to Perth towing the boat, turned into Alan having to drive a truck up instead. Julie and Mavis were instructed to follow with the boat. As it turned out, the boat was not properly connected on the hitch and soon disengaged. Alan sped on ahead, not once checking to see if all was well. Fortunately, the safety chains held the boat trailer in tow.

Alan later hauled Cooinda II all the way up to Shark Bay for a Boy's Own adventure.

## *The early morning dip*

In the 1960s when summer came, Alan was always up bright and ready for an early morning dip, or a swim and jog along Bunbury's Hungry Hollow beach, taking with him anyone in the household who couldn't put up a good resistance ploy. Never mind if the family were slow on the up-take, Alan had a volley of friends, fellow morning beach goers, who on occasion seemed keen to keep the momentum going by turning on and redirecting the big boom sprinkler on the front lawn onto the main bedroom window. That would always ensure his arrival on the said beach in good time.

## *Caravanning*

Caravanning adventures happened mainly in the August school holidays. How Alan did this with four daughters, each vying for position as the most unreasonable at any given time, was a feat to behold. But if Mavis had baked and packed a fruit cake, all was well. 'Fruit Cake Charlie is his name' was always chanted when Alan pulled over to the roadside for his morning tea stop.

Never one to be stationary very long, these caravanning trips tallied more hours spent in the car covering the many miles needed to reach his planned round-trip goals. Often the girls could only look forward to exploring the caravan park ablution blocks when they pulled in late, and before they left early the next morning. The joy of travelling together was always supported with sing-a-longs.

*Alan, up north, fixing the flat tyre on the caravan c.1965*

On one occasion, Alan was forced to leave the family who were stranded on the side of the road in the far north, near Wittenoom Gorge. The van was struck with a flat tyre and with no spare nor a way to fix it, Alan decided to leave the family with the van. He propped it up on a jack, and took off the punctured tyre and returned to the previous town. The girls couldn't go into the van, or so he said, but as time ticked on, thirst necessitated intervention. Together they all engineered Gail, the youngest, into the wounded caravan, by holding her horizontally towards the fridge to retrieve drinks.

Another drink-related story saw Alan, whilst caravanning up North with the family, pursuing a truck he recognised. The bloke, whose name was Aub, lived in Collie and bought a truck from Alan every year. Alan followed him right into the gravel pit where he was loading up. Reckoning it was hot work, Alan thought he'd offer him a cold beer but it turned out Aub had a small fridge in the front cab and immediately offered Alan a coldie. Apparently Aub drank a carton of beer throughout the day, because it was so hot up North.

Although the car and van often pointed North, Alan always made sure that Corrigin and the Smith family were on the radar.

Smiths and Parsons c.1963. The two families holidayed together for a number of years.
Front row; Susan Parsons, Suellen Smith, Ian Wells, Michael Smith
Middle row; Eleanor Parsons, Julie Parsons, Stephen Smith, Doug Wells
Back row; Mavis Parsons, Alan Parsons, Viv Smith, Betty Smith (baby Gail is sleeping)

The Smiths had a farming property at Kunjin and caravanning on their farm was always a highlight for the girls. More often than not, everything was timed around the Corrigin Show. Indeed, with everyone excited and dressed in their finery it was a wonderful opportunity to catch up with old friends and family. Alan's brother Brian and his wife Mary had remained in Corrigin to continue the farming tradition and raise their four children. Apart from anything else Mavis had an uncanny knack of winning on the chocolate wheel with the Smiths and each of the girls coming away with many glorious gifts. Likewise, the Smith family would haul their caravan to Bunbury after the harvest for the summer holidays and together the families would haunt the beaches, fishing spots, drive-ins, and the traveling carnivals that came to town after the festive season. Many meals were shared and most importantly Mavis and Alan were kept abreast of the goings on in Corrigin. Much joy and sadness was shared with the Smiths over the years as changes took place and the children grew up.

## *The games room*

The simple, three-bedroom brick and tile house in Mangles Street grew smaller as the family of six grew bigger and their interests expanded. Sleep-overs were often conducted in the garage, a structure well away from the house. The only toilet was on the end of a tiny, congested laundry where there was also a small shower recess, supposedly for rinsing off after the beach. But with five females bidding for lengthy solo time in the little bathroom, Alan found solitude in the laundry shower amidst its mountains of washing, and ignoring urgent calls for use of the little room at the end.

The laundry, kitchen, back door, lounge and passage all ran into a curious little room called the vestibule. The vestibule was where the ironing happened; it had close contact with the slow combustion stove where the two irons were initially placed to heat up. The hot irons could then be used in succession. Each item to be ironed was sprinkled with water and rolled tightly then placed in the wash basket to allow the fabric time to evenly absorb the damping down. The hot iron was applied over a protective dampened cloth, which was placed over each section of the garment to be pressed. Hot steam rose noisily with each press.

Eventually, a couple of mod cons found their way into the home and the ironing board continued its reign of terror in the vestibule, but now, attached to a power point, was the new electric iron. Mavis had ingeniously set it up this way so she could watch the new invention called the TV, while she ironed Alan's never-ending pile of shirts. The vision was distorted by first the terylene curtains on the glass doors, which screened the lounge room from the chaos in the vestibule, coupled by the 'snow' on the TV screen. However, the new electric iron was life-changing, although the tedious chore of the damping down routine continued into the '70s.

A rumpus room, huge laundry and Alan's own bathroom was added to the Mangles Street house in the '70s. The addition of a rumpus room expanded Alan's presence: the style of the day dictated that a bar and pool table were necessary in such a room. The bar became the place where Alan would get his daily half-hour laugh, while the pool table brought Alan closer to his family and offered a friendly outlet for associates to talk things over around a game of pool. The room, with its dramatic '70s bold red, geometric-patterned wallpaper and over-sized, hand-crafted kooky bar, was a great source of enjoyment for both family and friends. Alan tells of Aussie Cranston, a tyre dealer and champion pool player at the South West Club, who challenged a young Gail, then aged 14, to a game of pool. She cleaned him up. It is said Aussie never got over it.

*Mavis in costume for a Sol de Espana performance 1995*

In time, Mavis began to slowly encroach on this vast and spacious room with her costume manufacture for the South West Opera Company and Sol de Espana Spanish dance company productions. Mavis was often on stage but over time her real talents emerged in costume design. She became the South West Opera Company's official costume designer. Daughters Susan and Julie learnt a great deal about theatrical costume in this room. Much to the angst of the pool players in the family, the pool table made an excellent cutting table.

## *The Beach House*

Then came the Beach House and sojourns in Quindalup. The Beach House was a magical retreat during the mid-'80s to well into the '90s. The whole family continually enjoyed this spot with a parade of boyfriends, girlfriends, husbands and grandchildren, all able to reap the benefits of this little, unassuming cottage and its glorious surrounds maintained with its own bore and windmill.

*The beach house at Quindalup, taken from the path to the ocean.*
*A simple cottage backing onto Toby's inlet, with its own water tank and bore c.1990*

The original owner had, on occasion, accommodated the overworked Catholic nuns in the cottage by way of assisting their quest for rest and recreation. Alan saw no reason why this tradition could not continue when the family was not using the cottage. Alan met Sister Romanus and gave her a key. After a number of silly notes and keepsakes were exchanged they developed a great friendship. Her work in the community really impressed Alan and a solid respect for one another was established. She and the family have remained great friends ever since. When Sister Romanus moved to St John's in Subiaco she was well placed to support their daughter Eleanor during her encounter with cancer. Alan introduced Sister Romanus to his brother Brian and his Corrigin friend, Yvonne Matthews, during their periods of illness spent in the hospital, enabling her to support them through difficult times.

## Overseas and overland trips

Alan continued to beat sales records and win trips with his new dealership franchises. Mitsubishi sent him and Mavis off to Singapore, Canada and Italy, while Mercedes, of course, sent him to Germany. Automotive Holdings (for budget making) also sent them to Singapore, Thailand and Broome.

Boating trips with the boys became a popular past-time. Jack Best, although an unknown quantity at sea, owned a big boat capable of travelling up the coast to the Abrolhos Islands and up the coast they went. A 'fishing trip' it was called:

*Over the years I had several days of fun and fellowship on Jack Best's boat, Bold Venture. He built the boat in his workshops over a long period. The first trip was to Rottnest Island. We actually left after Rotary one Friday night, clambering on board at the Bunbury Harbour and heading out to sea in darkness. It was then we were told this was the 'shake down' trip. There were eleven guys, and thank heaven Dr Derm Foster was on board, as he was an experienced able-bodied seaman, who took over when the automatic pilot did not work correctly and we found ourselves heading straight out to sea. Eventually we got back to the west coast of Rotto but not until the next morning and after many other dramas.*

A 'Boy's Own' fishing trip up north. Back from right: Jimmy Hull, Rodney Johnston, Alan Parsons, Ian Johnston, Ted Court. Front: young Best, Ross Manolas, Dr Derm Foster c.1970s

*The dramas just kept on coming as the engine room continued filling up with water so we had to head around to Thompsons Bay. By then the engine room was flooded and the ship had to be grounded in Thompsons Bay. It was found that the pumps were pumping in, instead of out.*

*A year or two later, a trip to the Abrolhos Islands was planned. One group was to set sail from Bunbury, taking over six days. Another group was to fly up, and fish for five days, then another group was to fly up and sail Besty's boat home. I picked the middle group, which was very sensible. The sailing bit was apparently very hard and hazardous work. Many other trips were under taken but the two described were the most memorable.*

There is no doubt Alan needs to keep moving and is an instigator of this movement. Apart from family trips touring the state, in 1978 (a few days after Cyclone Alby), Mavis and Alan went to England on an extensive holiday with Rodney and Amy Johnston. This was the first of a short string of holiday adventures with the Johnstons.

*Alan with his catch, a Coral Trout and a Trevally on the Mackerel Islands August 1993*

*Rodney Johnston, Mavis Parsons, Amy Johnston and Alan Parsons on holiday in the UK, 1978*

The following year, Rodney said, 'A great holiday in the UK, what are we doing this year?' Little did Rodney know that Alan's love of road trips would take them across the continent. Alan had decided on a trip to Darwin, and had purchased a second-hand campervan and a tent. Amy used to say, 'Ladies don't go camping,' and wanted a hotel every second night, which of course didn't happen. A nightly game of cards saw to that and so they alternated between the tent and the Van.

Restless for the experience of the sea, Alan and Mavis set sail on the Queen Elizabeth II: its destination, Africa. Once they disembarked they went on safari to Victoria Falls and Zimbabwe. This was followed by a trip to Turkey in the late 1990s, which saw Mavis hospitalised after enjoying the exquisite Turkish cuisine in Istanbul. The food proved too salty, shooting up her blood pressure and creating an emergency situation. Together, Alan and Mavis trialled the Turkish medical system until all was calm. She was advised to avoid salty dishes, and back home they came.

# *A chip off the old block (of wood)*

The '80s was a chiselled decade in many ways, but who would have thought Alan would find his way to a woodworking class; his family certainly didn't. But with Graham Golding by his side off he went. They first looked at what the local tool shops had on offer and were encouraged to attend a one-day wood-turning workshop for a mere $95. They were requested to bring along a solid block of wood, about 20 x 20cm sq. and 30cm long. At the end of the day they both left with a little egg cup, valued at $95.

Unperturbed by the experience, Alan sought out backyard sales of second-hand woodworking equipment, which slowly made its way into the Mangles Street garage. Being 'fully equipped' turned into hoarding massive amounts of potential timbers awaiting transformation. He and Graham were no doubt quietly competing with each other when they both decided to attend a TAFE night class with some of their mates. It's hard to imagine what earnest nonsense went on there, but the revelation that you didn't need nails anymore was one of the surprising outcomes. A range of 'Jolly Green Giant' furniture began to emerge. The recipients, his daughters, coined the name. Often painted a deep forest green were towel racks, planters, bars stools, book cases, workshop shelving, cupboards, coffee tables and eventually his beautiful full-sized dining tables. The new Hard as Nails glue soon copped the 'thumbs down' as bar stools began to fall to pieces. This tale was taken from Julie's diaries in tribute to Alan's mother, her grandmother:

> *During the woodworking craze, I was lucky enough to be able to influence and even work with my father on a few pieces I had designed for art exhibitions. Once we developed a wonderful working relationship I realised anything was possible, and with the theme of a group show* Drawing from the Past *approaching, the sky opened up and out fell the notion of something wonderful. My father's mother's drawers.*
> 
> *I had grown up fascinated with a piece of furniture in my Grandmother's house. Alma later gave it to me when she moved to a unit in the '70s. I cherished it*

ill vii: Alma the Hat Box Drawers, 1995.
A homage to Alan's mother Alma Parsons.
Design and finish by Julie Parsons,
construction by Alan Parsons with Julie.
Size: 180 x 60 x 60cm

*dearly. Alma kept all her hats and handbags in the drawers, along with her most precious family photos. She had inherited the set of drawers and proudly told me they were made during the Great Depression from hat boxes and old packing case timber. The three, now lidless, hat boxes were covered in glorious, deep musky pink, floral fabric. I loved looking at that fabric, more than anything in her house. The hat boxes were encased in a simple but crude timber framework, stained with a dark varnish. During one of my house moves in the early 1990s the hat box drawers made their way to my sister Susan's home. She saw what I did not, and promptly removed the rotting fabric and re-covered them in a blue, miniature floral print fabric, thus claiming them as her own. There was no way I could retrieve them. But now, with the opportunity to recreate them firmly in my mind, I completely reinvented them in homage to my Grandmother.*

*Together, Alan and I built the framework of the life-size piece as a tribute to his mother. We then constructed each of the drawers, including the two top breast drawers. We also made a timber jewellery box in the shape of a cheeky full-sized head to complete the portrait.*

*The head had hidden pull-out drawers behind the eyes, mouth and neck for keeping trinkets. The head would also support hats. We made and attached arms, one of which was to carry handbags and baskets. The front legs sported a stunning pair of high heel shoes, also fashioned in timber through our collaborative efforts. I took it all to my studio where I painted and dressed, or rather covered, each drawer with a fabric vaguely reminiscent of the original. I then accessorised according to my Grandmother's taste. Remembering the touch of her gloved fingers squeezing my little girl cheeks I added gloves. With these slight but impressive changes to the design, together we bonded, chatting about the memories which surfaced. I had originally titled the work My Father's Mother's Drawers but it soon became Alma the hat box drawers. The piece was initially exhibited at its intended art show held at Bunbury Regional Art Galleries, followed by an invitation to show it at another exhibition in Perth, representing South West artists, called South West South Best.*

*Alan learnt a lot about the power of guesstimates and I learnt a great deal about him and his relationship with his mother. We became very close.*

Slowly, with each house move, interest dwindled and bit by bit the wood and woodworking equipment was sold off or given away and replaced with a bike.

## *Cycling the South West*

The rekindled passion for bike riding occurred at the beach house with all the family keeping bikes there. The bike was Alan's choice of transport to the Dunsborough shops for the daily paper, bread and milk. All the skills he had acquired as a young boy riding the corrugations and delivering papers returned. He always rode with the confidence and look of a young boy, even into his eighties.

*Alan and a mate leading the pack of the Fearless Free-Wheelers in 1992*

Alan joined the over-50s cycle group in the '90s and proceeded to challenge himself and the group. After all, he was an 'in front kinda guy'. After a few years of being in the bikey gang, which included a couple of charity rides to Perth, Alan formed his own gang. Graham Golding, Wally Jones, Fred Clarke, Les Pike, Ross Bedford and Bob Slee featured among them. The favourite ride was to Australind for coffee and back. Electric bikes made an appearance in the 2000s and Alan eventually succumbed and procured himself a fine machine in 2015. The phrase 'deadly treadly' took on a new meaning when he began clocking up the kilometres and travelling at speed. Wally Jones claims, 'He is hard to keep up with these days'. There have been a few tumbles, but with no loss of enthusiasm he continues to ride along the ocean-front most days.

# *Then along came golf*

Playing regular sport could never be on Alan's busy radar, so when an opportunity to play golf presented itself, he could never guarantee to arrive at the course in time for tee off. Besides, golf was not a game he had considered. He had enjoyed hard and fast ball games like tennis and squash in the past and that made sense given his time constraints, but golf was an unsuitable institution. Nevertheless, he was drawn in when Capel's new golf course was being established. The club had organised a number of busy-bees and needed a tractor. Alan sold them a good second-hand model and got involved with building the course. He was invited to play but try as he might, he was unable to arrive on time to play a game. As time passed, circumstances changed, allowing time to be on his side. Some mates lured him to the Bunbury golf course for golf lessons.

The golfing buddies, who were not dissimilar to the bikey gang, formed a loose group, meeting regularly, but without commitment, allowing a last-minute cancellation. The core group consisted of: Graham Golding, who was still a farmer, albeit an emu farmer; Fred Clarke, a farmer; Ross Bedford, a former employee of Alan's; and Les Pike, a butcher. The group was like a rolling snowball gathering other players who came and went along the way. New members caught in the momentum were Wally Jones and Bob Slee. Anyone playing solo was immediately invited to join them but not without fun and games, as the group had developed their own unique scoring system.

In this way, they gained some unusual associations like Smithy, a retired overseas engineer from BP oils and Marinus, a sea captain from Norway. Marinus would bring his merchant ship into Bunbury's port regularly, so he appeared on the course often enough to be included in the main group. As walking the course got steadily more difficult, Graham with his hip and knee replacements, and Alan now well into the latter part of his 80s, began to hire a golf buggy (which conjures up visions of Fred Flintstone and Barney Rubble). Naturally, handicaps began to drop and it became the comradeship, tales and coffee, which bound them.

*Front of A&M Trucks in Forrest Avenue showing the line-up of brand new trucks, 1985*

## CHAPTER TEN

## *"The funny thing was, the harder I worked the luckier I became"*
### *Alan Parsons*

### But wait he's back

In 1981 Alan sold the A&M Parsons dealership to David Nicholas, the 'Aspro King', from Melbourne. Nicholas was a bit of a cowboy who wanted to get his company into the car business in Perth, via a small one in the country. They ultimately achieved their aim when they went on to buy Winterbottoms and Sydney Atkinson Motors.

Alan was invited to become a director of Sydney Atkinson Motors in 1982. His duties included making decisions about the direction of the company. It was a public company and people could buy shares in it; as a director Alan signed documents allowing this. The company, however, was not transparent in its dealings and Alan felt his values and theirs were on different courses, so he resigned before the year was up.

Even though Alan was engaged in his role as a director for Sydney Atkinson Motors, he had already been dabbling for a year in real estate, through Steere and Clarke. Being too young for retirement, Alan had joined the Steere and Clarke real estate agency, selling farms or trying to, he says. His old mate, Rodney Johnston, was trying hard to sell Alan both the concept and the real estate agency but Alan was not sure it was his thing.

At this time, Rodney Johnston, his long-time friend, and Alan formed a stronger bond. Rodney was older and had lost his son. Alan was younger and had lost his father. Alan had never felt truly appreciated by his father and when he died, it seems that he and his friend Rodney worked out a way to heal their losses and fill the void.

Alan worked in real estate for two years, before reconsidering his options. As he still owned the premises in Forrest Avenue, where he had established A&M Parsons, he made the decision to open another dealership in 1983, this time calling it the A&M Truck Centre, thereby attracting offers of a dealership with Mitsubishi, Mercedes and International Trucks.

All this came about because R. Moore and Sons, an engine reconditioning company with considerable success under their belt, had taken on two truck franchises in Perth. These were going well so they opened one up in Blair Street, Bunbury. However, as the Bunbury office was proving unsuccessful, Bobby Moore invited Alan to work for them to get their business in Bunbury back on track.

Surprisingly, within 12 months the two Perth franchises were not doing well either and R. Moore and Sons offered Alan the Bunbury franchise, so that they could move out of that area altogether. Alan picked it up and ran with it. He also picked up their salesman Wally Jones. In Alan's words:

> *I did not enjoy the real estate industry and when Bob Moore of R. Moore and Sons approached me to take over and manage his truck dealership in Bunbury in about 1982, I said yes.*
>
> *Bob had the franchise in Perth to sell and service Mitsubishi and UD trucks and had opened a branch in Bunbury. In the meantime, IHC had gone bankrupt as I forecast.*
>
> *The Melbourne people, Hoile and Co., who were running my old business, had destroyed the Bunbury dealership and had walked away from the lease of the former A&M Parsons premises on Forrest Ave. I had then leased the premises to Barry Myles, the Shell dealer for twelve months, while the Shell Oil Company built new premises in Bunbury for him. In that period, Bob Moore gave me the*

> franchises in Bunbury and sold out of them in Perth. He lost a lot of money in the dealerships.
>
> At that stage, I had two franchises and suitable premises so I put it altogether and opened up as A&M Truck Centre in our old address in Forrest Ave. I rounded up some of my old employees and brought Wally Jones with me. Then I got the Iveco and Mercedes truck franchises and away we went.
>
> In the meantime, David Nicholas and his henchmen had acquired three dealerships in Perth which tipped the car marketing in Perth on its head.
>
> I was offered a directorship in Sydney Atkinson as they were short of people, so I became a director in the biggest car franchise in Perth. That lasted four months until I found they were juggling the sales tax on new cars. I resigned immediately having only been to about three meetings. That was when I eventually met David Nicholas.
>
> Vern Wheatley and Automotive Holdings then acquired the mess. Nicholas ended up in jail, and his two henchmen disappeared.

Alan reopened the doors in Forrest Ave, having recruited some of his former staff such as the brilliant foreman, Ian Clifton, and two or three other mechanics and parts personnel. He also located his excellent former office manager, Jan Sullivan and together with Wally Jones in sales they were underway. Wally Jones says of those heady days and his experience of Alan's leadership:

> I was impressed by Alan's forthright way of lifting truck sales and his pleasant way of communicating with staff. I learnt a lot about sales techniques during that time. Under Alan's guidance we built up a great dealership (along with a solid friendship). The eight years working with Alan were most pleasant and rewarding.

*The Parts counter with Dean Armstrong, a former workshop mechanic who was injured when a truck fell off a jack onto his leg. When Dean was well enough Alan transferred him to the Parts department where he excelled.*

As soon as it became apparent Parsons was back in business with his resurrected Forrest Ave workshop, he was offered the Mercedes truck franchise, followed by the International Trucks franchise (IVECO). By then, International Farm Machinery had been separated from International Trucks and established as two separate franchises.

It seemed that luck was on his side yet again, as the business took off and went speedily towards another successful dealership, but Alan humbly says it was because his biggest asset was his team of employees.

# A&M TRUCK CENTRE

Bunbury-based truck and tractor specialists, A&M Trucks, holds an enviable position as Western Australia's largest rural truck dealership. Under founding chairman and ongoing partner, Alan Parsons, A&M Trucks has sold in excess of 130 trucks in a trading year. A&M now holds Western Australia's only rural Mercedes Benz truck franchise and is an appointed dealer for International Harvester Trucks, and the full range of Mitsubishi heavy commercial vehicles.

One of A&M Trucks' strongest performances is in the area of service and parts for International trucks. With clientele drawn from agriculture, mining and other industries in the rich south west regions of W.A., A&M Trucks has continued to expand to satisfy the demands of both large and small fleet operators. The company is based in busy Forrest Avenue, Bunbury, occupying almost one hectare of land and employing 13 people.

The increasing market share enjoyed by Mercedes Benz and Mitsubishi in the medium to heavy truck market indicates an even more vital role for A&M Trucks in the future.

A&M Trucks is an essential link to many rural-based industries for which road transport is often the only means of transporting goods and services.

**ALAN PARSONS**
*General Manager*

*A&M Truck Centre article from* Linking the Strength of Western Australia's Largest Automotive Group, *1987 (courtesy of Automotive Holdings Ltd).*

# At the close of business

In *Wheels of Fortune* by Colin Rockman, a book describing the history of Automotive Holdings, Alan Parsons is described as 'a delightful chap for truck division staff to work with'. The author later says, 'Dave Simpson (of Skipper Trucks) and Alan Parsons struck up a great working relationship'. This positive liaison lead to Skipper Trucks expanding their business in the South West.

Upon reflection, a past connection made during the Great Depression between Syd Wheatley, the instigator of Automotive Holdings, and the Parsons family, demands attention. Back then, Alan's father, Cliff, could buy a truck from Syd under good terms, a fortunate turn of events for the struggling young Cliff Parsons. Owning the truck enabled him to work on the Wellington Dam Project and thereby support his young family during Australia's biggest crisis to date. In 1993, A&M Truck Centre was sold to Automotive Holdings and Alan retired from this business.

*The premises with Alan's well-known number plate BY 714 on his car parked in its familiar spot. Alan received the plate in 1962 and kept it to enable people to identify him on his travels throughout the South West. The Bunbury City Council had been after his plate for years, in order to finish their suite of plates numbered in the early 700s. The number plate BY 714, remains in the family to this day.*

## Summary of Alan's selling career

When Alan left the farm, he became an International Harvester Company salesman for the dealership in Bunbury, followed by ownership of the business and dealership manager. He worked eleven zones from Waroona to Darkan and Augusta. When International went into receivership world-wide, he moved into real estate before returning to a dealership, this time in trucks. He took on Mitsubishi, Mercedes and IVECO franchises. He sold an astounding number of trucks. Alan reckons from 1960 to 1993 they sold 3,500 new and used trucks, making it one of the biggest regional dealerships in WA and on occasion in Australia.

In an article written by Bill Cranny for Western Transport, 1989 p.43-45, Cranny describes Alan as having sold the business in 1980 and reacquiring it in 1984. In it, Alan says of the second operation, that it was time to devote themselves single-mindedly to the truck market. Working from a single franchise was no longer viable. The industry had changed and A&M Truck Centre was now franchised to sell Mitsubishi, International Harvester and Mercedes Benz trucks.

Alan's approach was to make sure his staff understood the value of eyeballing the client, with one staff member being quoted as saying "you can't sell trucks sitting around the office". And yet there was also another level to the commitment and stability of Alan's key staff members. His manager, service manager, business manager and sales manager were all minor shareholders in the company.

Cranny also writes that surprisingly, trade for A & M Truck Centre did not suffer from any measurable seasonal fluctuations, saying Alan Parsons put this down to the diversity of commercial activity in the State's South West. There was mining, all kinds of agriculture, logging and timber milling.

Quoting Alan in the 1989 article, Cranny writes:

*Today, every truck is specialised. The days are long gone when in the South West an eight ton petrol truck could be a tipper, flat top or whatever and with Mitsubishi, International Harvester and Mercedes Benz we are well equipped to meet the need for everything from a light truck to an all-wheel heavy weight for off road logging operations trucks.*

Advertisement in feature article in Western Transport, 1989, p.43-45
Note: Wally Jones (pictured), Alan's salesman for eight years and long-time friend thereafter

During his dealership days, Alan had successfully convinced the management of the International Harvester Company of the wisdom of establishing, a 'Dealer Council' to represent and listen to the dealers Australia wide. This they did. Alan says it was a proud day.

## Commercial properties

The part of Forrest Avenue where Alan's premises was located had evolved into a reputable business centre, particularly for vehicles. Paul Vukelic owned the car dealership two doors down the road, so when the premises between Alan and Paul came up for sale, the two had an idea. This idea grew into a partnership and eventually a reality, as together in 1970 they purchased the central shed, which housed Bunbury Glass Works. Alan bought Paul out about ten years later. By then, Paul Vukelic had sold his car yard and had moved into Blair Street (behind Forrest Avenue), which was attracting better passing traffic. At this point Alan owned nearly three acres in Forrest Avenue.

In 1985 Peters Ice Creameries approached Alan to build refrigerated premises for their purposes. Peters did not want to own the property, their preference being to lease the premises back. Alan obliged. He approached Paul Vukelic to partner him in this venture also.

*Building Peters Ice Creameries 1992*

Alan borrowed 1.2 million from the bank and Jack Best built it to Peters specifications and plans. Peters paid monthly, ensuring the loan was paid off in just eight years. This time, Paul bought Alan out about ten years later.

In the meantime, Alan had bought the ANZ Bank building in South Bunbury through A&M Parsons. The ANZ manager had called Alan one day to tell him the bank was going to sell their premises and Alan said, 'You finance me and I'll buy it', and they did. Alan did not put any money towards it at all, but it was paid off in about seven years.

While that was happening Alan, again partnering with Paul Vukelic, purchased some shops in Victoria Street opposite the Burlington Hotel. These were bought at around the same time and sold about five years later.

In the summer of the 1990s, whilst holidaying at the family's beach house in Quindalup, Alan noticed things were changing in the area with its increase in popularity. The old original caravan park next door was struggling. Alan was alert to this and together with Graham Golding, who was a cattle, dairy and emu farmer and emu oil developer, whom Alan knew through business and Rotary, looked it over. Graham was also prone to holiday in the Dunsborough area and was keen on a partnered venture. They did their homework and discussed the possibilities that might eventuate if they built holiday units on the property.

Golding and Parsons soon decided to purchase the park and began to redevelop it into units and apartments. With the partnership forged and doing well, they then decided to sink the profits they achieved into a new venture. They bought a Rockingham office block, which they owned outright. After about ten years Golding and Alan divided the ownership to each, independently own an office area.

Alan has always said trust is the number one element in business, and that you need to show your trust early in the piece. Graham and Jenny Golding echoed this when asked about their experience with Alan and Mavis in their partnered ventures:

'They have been great partners in business and we have always felt very comfortable, trusting completely in one another's integrity.'

# *The return to the land*

Along the way Alan explored farm properties and cattle-growing markets. He first purchased 100 acres in the Ferguson Valley. This beautiful property had a stream but was largely on a steep hillside. The family was taken on picnics during weekends while Alan dashed about fixing fences and making general improvements, all the while dodging friendly cattle he was running on the property. Within a couple of years, he had sold it and bought 100 acres on the flats in Dardanup.

The Dardanup farm was partly cleared but still held scattered stands of tall, open woodland (predominantly WA Peppermint, Marri, Jarrah and Banksia) as well as some coastal plain scrub and vegetation in the remaining wetland area. Most of the wetland on this farm was cleared and grassed for cattle, which meant that after rains the cattle struggled to find dry ground. On this property chain sawing, cutting up and then burning the fallen, dead wood seemed to be the call of the day. Even though a fine set of cattle yards allowing trucks easy access for loading and unloading cattle was a very appealing asset, and the property was closer to Bunbury enabling quick checks on his cattle, it really was not suitable for growing good market cattle.

After a few years Alan sold the Dardanup property and purchased 130 acres at Nannup on the Blackwood River. The cattle yards were strong, solid affairs and the land was pristine, making it perfect for his growing cattle projects. Again, all the family travelled there, some with husbands and children, and camped by the exquisite Blackwood River, a wonderland of natural vegetation, while chores were carried out. In time, keeping an eye on this property became onerous and it too was sold. Alan says of these ventures: 'None of it was very profitable but it was a good release for me from the dealership, plus, I think some fun was had between us all.'

When Alan sold the Forrest Avenue properties, he invested in an apartment at the newly revived and renovated Silo apartments, on the shoreline of Koombana Bay. The apartments adjoined a hotel and were close to city amenities. Alan originally imagined this to be a future solution for down-sizing purposes, but it has yet to happen.

*Alan at the cattle yards on the Blackwood River property at the finish of a busy weekend day*

## *New mates*

Soon a new wave of mates' names wafted through: Ted Court, Dave Simpson, Graham Golding, Paul Vukelic and of course the continuation of Jack Best and Rodney Johnston ... to name a few. When Graham and Jenny Golding speak of their friendship with Alan and Mavis it is clear the bonds of business came from a respected and valued friendship:

> *We have enjoyed so many happy times with Mavis and Alan and value their friendship deeply. Alan is an adventurous and successful achiever and Mavis is talented and interested in many facets of the artistic world. They complement one another well.*

Likewise, when former employee Wally Jones retired he was invited to join Alan, Graham and the rest of the guys for weekly Boy's Own golfing and cycling mornings. So that the wives were not separated from their friendship, many social occasions were organised. Wally and Gwen Jones say some of the varied outings included holidays in caravans, lunches, and a chat over a glass of wine on the home front.

## *Community Contributions*

There is no doubt Alan is a key mover and shaker in raising money for community ventures. His sense of compassion would not allow him to turn away from those in need as he began his Bunbury work through Rotary, delivering Christmas packages to struggling families. Disillusioned with the attitudes of some of these folk, he turned to bigger ventures, which would benefit the wider community.

Alan donated substantial money to building the Hay Park Recreation Centre, which began in the late 1970s but has since been upgraded and is now called the South West Sports Centre — one of the biggest facilities outside of Perth, owned and operated by the City of Bunbury. Alan also gave substantial money to the retirement apartments managed by the Masonic lodge.

# The Norm Payton debacle

A crisis swept Bunbury and its surrounds in 1986 when investors realised their involvement in Norm Payton's finance firm was fouled. Norm Payton was a pioneer in the hire purchase industry, providing hire purchase opportunities mainly to the country folk of the South West. The trouble impacted 2,499 investors.

Norm Payton's faulty decisions were caused by his personal purchases of properties. There were no shareholders as such; Norm paid higher rates of interest to his investors. People willingly took the higher risk of investing with him for higher returns. As his playboy antics came to light, so did the realisation that he had fouled some $26m.

In 1972 an enquiry was set up in the form of a Western Australian Honorary Royal Commission into 'hire purchase' and other agreements. At the time, there was a great deal of concern about what was happening to enable easy purchases of goods, but which had long term complications for the purchaser who had gone into debt. Norm Payton's finance firm was investigated and although the reveal was appalling at the time, the full scope of the problem did not come to light until 1986.

As a consequence, a committee of concerned professionals and citizens was formed, consisting of an accountant, a bank manager, some farmers and Alan Parsons. A reviewer was appointed who worked for the committee. Norm Payton's son, Ross, who had been educated in the UK, and his wife Janet arrived in Bunbury to help return investors' monies and confidence.

To recoup and return the lost monies to the investors, Ross entered the rural community like no other. Alan had never seen anything like it and confesses that it was too big to wrap his head around, so he had to put his trust in Ross. Ross became the anchor-man on the committee. He set up massive farming concerns, which were able to send up to two semi-trailers of pigs to market at a time. Another project Ross initiated was to purchase a huge number of rams from South Australia to breed with up to 10,000 ewes.

Finally, on 28 December 1993 the front page of *The West Australian* carried the headline: $26m paid back with interest.

## Trusts and Foundations

Alan also laid down the community foundation work behind the Val Lishman Foundation and the Rodney Johnston Memorial Trust. The following is a description from the Foundation's website (2017):

> *The Lishman Health Foundation was established by health professionals and Rotarians in 1997, as the Val Lishman Health Research Foundation. It was set up to honour the inspirational work of Dr Val Lishman, the first specialist surgeon in the South West region of Western Australia. The Foundation is guided by Dr Lishman's example of selfless service and concern for holistic health.*

The Val Lishman Foundation unanimously made Alan a life member in September 2011. He was the first member to be granted life membership, chiefly because of his outstanding fundraising efforts. The South Western Times newspaper on 15 September 2011, carried an article, Humble Fundraiser Recognised, quoting the foundation's executive officer Richard Jackson who said that Alan Parsons, 'is a very humble individual'. It seems Alan's business prowess and capacity as business advisor influenced local businesses to support the foundation. Jackson observed that Alan encouraged the businesses to use their success to benefit the foundation. The article ends with Jackson adding; 'Alan Parsons says he was "just helping out a worthy cause"'.

Val Lishman was indeed the first qualified surgeon in Bunbury. The research was specifically aimed at health issues in the South West. Dr Graham Fisher approached Alan for assistance in raising more money for the Foundation. Graham's focus at the time was cancer research in the South West region. Alan obliged and set about raising over $200,000, with the biggest single cheque contribution being a whopping $60,000. Well done Alan.

# Community Theatre Groups

Throughout Alan's married life he shared his home with costume design drawings, music, design research material, puppets, stage props, and costumes in various stages of construction. Not to mention the constant but varied forms of rehearsals. Mavis and all the girls enjoyed diverse adventures into the theatrical world both on and off stage. He knew first-hand how difficult theatre practise was in Bunbury with a 'make do' approach and complete lack of competent facilities.

Alan and Mavis had travelled considerably and had been to a number of big shows, both international and national. They had seen how professional theatres brought a vibrancy to communities, so Alan was mentally well situated to 'act', so to speak. The community began to drive change in the late '70s, with the loss of the Railway Institute and its stage, forcing the Bunbury Musical Comedy Group to find a new home. As Mavis had been both performer and chief costume designer with the group for a number of productions, Alan knew all about the impact first hand. The arts community pushed hard for a regional theatre and somewhere to stage high quality, travelling shows and performances.

*International opera singer Terry Greene, a mover and shaker for quality changes to theatre in Bunbury. Terry expertly taught singing at her baby grand piano then took those singers to new heights of production in Bunbury c.1990*

The emergence of a fledgling South West Opera Company under the auspices of international opera singer Miss Terry Greene saw Mavis singing opera again. Terry's colourful, larger-than-life presence began to fill the Mangles Street house as she increasingly sought Mavis' expertise with costume design and construction. Alan watched on helplessly as his beloved games room disappeared under the weight of heavy opera costumes, progressively becoming an operatic sweat shop.

*Mavis (in black gown) with costumed South West Opera Company singers for promotion for The Merry Widow c.1990s*

This was a covert call to action and by the late 1980s, when the arts community and the city council came to an agreement, Alan became involved with the fund-raising committee. The following is taken from the Bunbury Regional Entertainment Centre website in 2017:

> *In the late 1980s, this proposal was injected with new life as a steering committee was formed. The committee gauged public opinion, developed concept plans and investigated the potential for theatre developments.*
>
> *From this, a successful fundraising committee was formed, which raised $2.2 million and generated much-needed corporate and community support. The committee relied on donations from local families, businesses and individuals; these generous contributions have enabled BREC to mature into the highly reputable venue it is today. We acknowledge these tremendous efforts and the local support South West residents have provided us over the years; our growth is only made possible through your continued commitment.*

## *Bunbury Regional Entertainment Centre*

Regarding the role Alan played in establishing the Bunbury Regional Entertainment Centre, he recalled how it came about:

> *In the late 1980s, during the early days of planning the Bunbury Regional Theatre, a fundraising professional was brought across to Western Australia from the eastern states to get Bunbury started on raising funds for a regional entertainment centre. This fund-raising professional approached me to raise $400,000 for the project.*
>
> *'What me? I'm running a trucking dealership – far too busy!'*
>
> *Well he talked me round and described the way to raise the money. He suggested getting together a team. Team members were asked to donate towards the theatre before they set about approaching their own associates and contacts, or anyone whom they believed would be willing to contribute.*

*It required a weekly early morning meeting, held before business hours commenced. At these meetings, each evaluated their own individual target towards achieving the final goal of $400,000 in 16 weeks. My job was to mentor those who requested assistance and to prod and check on others to see how they were doing, if necessary. Sometimes, if required, I went with a team member to support them in their experience of building and how to ask for donations. Towards the end of the allocated time a rather humorous situation arose when I offered to go with solicitor, Campbell Young. Campbell had found the imposition of asking for donations awkward. We went to see two or three people in the Burekup, Brunswick area and emerged victorious. However, on our way home through Australind, I saw Joe Catalano on the balcony of his home having a beer, as was his practise after a hard day's work. I twigged he would be a worthy donor, so we turned around and headed up his driveway.*

*Campbell immediately panicked and said, 'I can't possibly approach Joe because I am acting against him in court next week'. Joe too immediately panicked asking the question, 'Why would a truck dealer be calling on him bringing a solicitor?'*

*After the initial shock and a congenial beer enjoyed on the balcony, I was told to call into his office on Tuesday; I did and there was a cheque for $10,000!*

*We successfully raised the allocated figure, and as a committee we exceeded the required amount, raising $440,000.*

With the theatre built, and up and running in 1990, Alan and Mavis were frequent supporters both through the stage door and the foyer. Some 23 years later in 2013, extensions began and Alan saw another opportunity to contribute, this time through the placement of public art.

In 2014, Alan, through the Rodney Johnston Memorial Trust and alongside Rotary, contributed to the acquisition, and installation process, of a major artwork in the foyer of the new addition to the Bunbury Regional Entertainment Centre. Alan was again the mover and shaker, which saw the establishment of a committee to follow through with the protocol required to place public art in a public building.

Bunbury Regional Theatre Inc. 1.5 Million Fund: Official Launch 23rd May 1989
Standing from left: Alan Parsons (Key Gifts Chairman), Paul Vukelic (Chairman Governing Body), Dr Ern Manea (Mayor of Bunbury), Hon. David Smith (MLA, Minister for the South West), Ross Ranson (Chairman Building Fund), Max Brett (Community Gifts Chairman), Merv Waugh (Major Gifts Chairman). Seated left to right; Dawn Fraser (OBE, MP), Dawn Smith (Program Director), Hon. David Parker (MLA, Deputy Premier & Minister for the Arts). Photo courtesy Bunbury Regional Entertainment Centre

## *Exchange tours between Bunbury businessmen and Corrigin farmers*

Beginning in 2014, when in his mid-80s, Alan developed a concept of enrichment where he aimed to raise awareness of farming practises and in turn bring the same to family owned South West Urban Enterprises and so grow a relationship between farmers and city dwellers. He thought that many people in Bunbury had scant knowledge of the way farming had changed, and with Alan's previous experience of farming in the Wheatbelt some 60 years prior, the concept of an investigative venture appealed to him. A farm tour coupled with advancements in farm machinery (that had increased in size and value), represented an opportunity to showcase these advancements in farming to the city folk of Bunbury.

Alan organised a bus load of Bunbury businessmen and South West farmers (some retired). He had a good Corrigin contact in retired farm machinery dealer, Greg Humphries. Humphries set up a program, which fell across two or three days during the December harvest, to include harvesting procedures.

*Long-time friend Graham Golding possibly contemplating Alan's contribution to the construction the Gorge Rock Pool during 1956. c.2009*

Alan also considered that many farmers had no idea what was going on in a big city like Bunbury. He reckoned he knew how to remedy this and set about organizing a bus to bring interested farmers to Bunbury. Hotel rooms were booked for their stay and a program of visits to various family-owned businesses was organised. Alan decided that as Corrigin farming concerns were family-owned, it would be beneficial to exchange ideas with family-owned South West businesses. Visits were organised to horticultural export companies, owned or commenced by family-owned businesses, expansive dairy farms, Harvey Fresh and Piacentini & Son, a transport and earth moving company (now employing up to 700 people). This was not always so, as Alan explained:

*When I arrived in Bunbury, in 1959, Albert Piacentini lived in a humpy out in the Ferguson Valley. He had a bulldozer, which enabled him to clear farms. I sold him a second-hand truck in 1961 to cart loads of timber to his sawmill. When mining started in Capel he got the contract to do the earthworks, which is where the Piacentini family success began. They now enjoy mining operations around Australia and parts of Africa and this is still a family-owned business.*

*Some Bunbury people would get on the bus with the Corrigin farmers to take the South West tour of diverse industries because they were unaware of the operations occurring in their own territory.*

*One year, I included the desalination plant in Binningup. This certainly aroused much interest as the tour was joined by many South West people. All in all, the exchanges have been successful in many ways.*

*The most rewarding aspect was the great fellowship, which would radiate from the Wheatbelt jaunts, and likewise when the Corrigin farmers came to Bunbury during their quiet months around March and April. So far, the exchange trips have been undertaken four times.*

The costs were always well calculated with any subsequent leftovers being donated to the Royal Flying Doctor Service. Alan chose RFDS because his first grandson was saved when Julie, his eldest daughter, was flown to Perth in premature labour. Her son Rad was born at 25 weeks gestation, weighing just 810 grams and has survived well and healthy to this day. Had he been born in Bunbury in 1981 he would have died.

## Back to the homefront

No one thought Alan and Mavis would ever move from their brick and tile home in Mangles Street, but everyone knew Mavis wanted to. They had expanded their home around the family and with the empty nest echoing there came the urge to move to something different.

The two moves, from 101 Mangles Street to Dunstan Street, then finally to 5 The Strand, were big events. The first move involved clearing out unused tools and keepsakes from the farm. The second move saw unproductive hobbies cleared away. But neither of these clear outs managed to remove a set of bowls, which remained unused in their original 1950s case. While the Mangles Street house was very much home for some 30 years, once the girls had moved on, Alan and Mavis decided to improve their living arrangements for their retirement. In 1994, they moved to Dunstan St. It had a pool and seemed to be a good choice, at the time but it turned out to be a transition home. Just prior to 2000, an opportunity came along that could not be refused; Alan and Mavis leapt at it.

This opportunity was to purchase a house block on Koombana Bay, which had just been opened up along The Strand, at Marlston Hill in the city centre. Incredibly, in the early days of Bunbury, this beachfront land had been the ad hoc camping grounds for Collie folk during the hot summer months. Many a family loaded up vehicles with all the necessities of home, including kerosene fridges, and headed to the coast. Once set up in the makeshift camping grounds, they embraced the view. Stretching out into the Bay was the original timber wharf, from which the town's port activities took place, and on which families took up their positions to catch fish for their evening meal.

As Alan's maternal family were Collie people in the early 1900s, it is fair to say they too made the trip down to the Bay. Perhaps they joined the happy campers, travelling in Bert's converted bus or truck, no doubt with their kerosene fridge on the back. Alan and Mavis Parsons' house on The Strand, may well stand in close proximity to where the 1901 Jetty Baths corrugated iron tea rooms once stood.

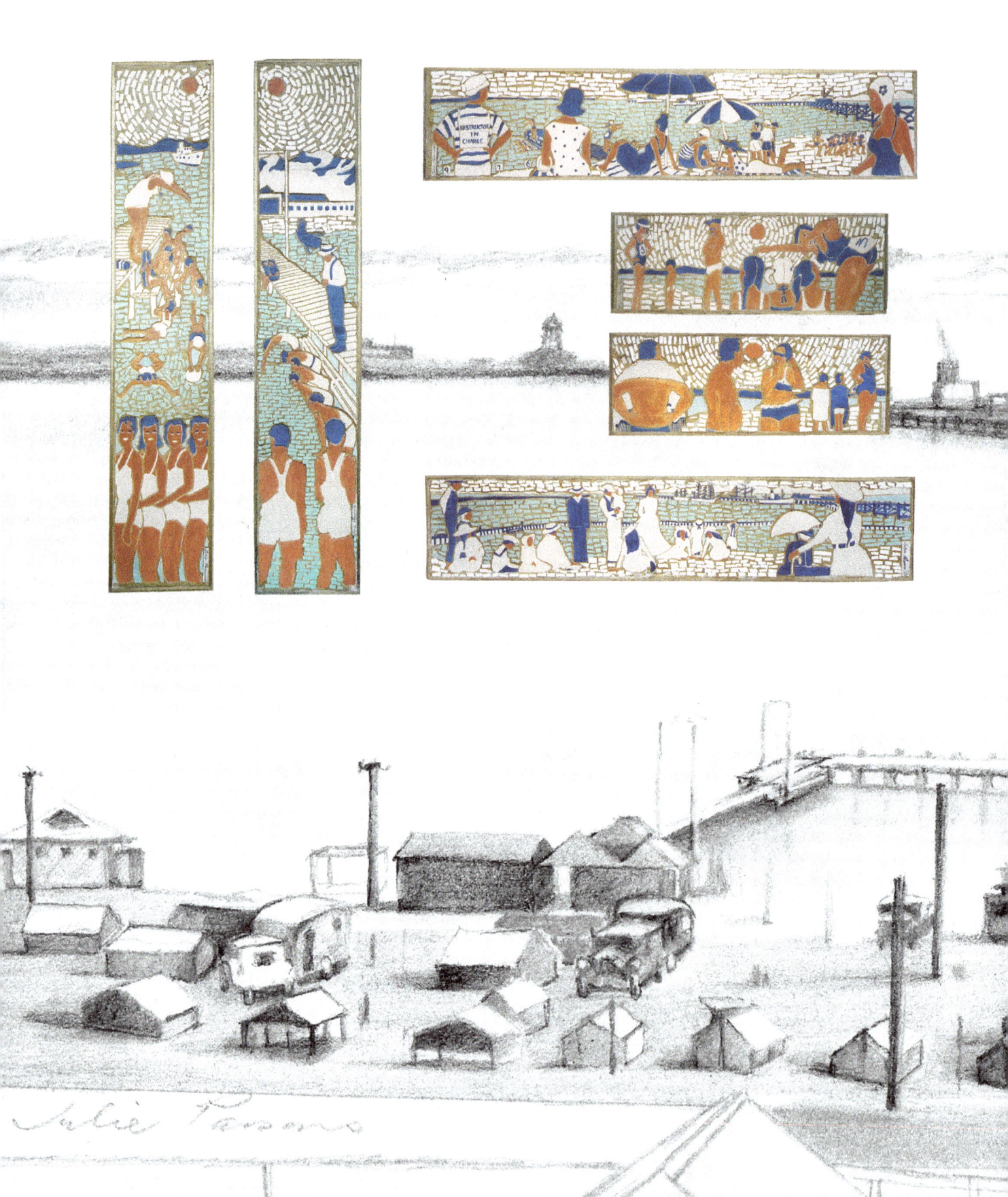

*ill viii:* INSET LEFT Commissioned hand painted mosaics by Julie Parsons, set in the limestone seawalls around Marlston Hill, which depict one century of swimming lessons at the Jetty Baths. All of Alan and Mavis' daughters learnt to swim at the Jetty Baths, each lesson always followed by a milkshake at the milk bar on the edge of town.

*ill ix:* Drawing (detail) of the Jetty Baths in 1940. A view from a sand dune which once stood immediately behind Mavis and Alan's new home in The Strand. Tents can be seen positioned in an organised manner unlike the early 1900s when Collie holiday goers would set up their famous Tent City temporarily to escape the heat up on the Collie Hills. Taken from a photograph in the Port's history collection.
Artist Julie Parsons 2001.

From such a humble beginning of their life together, in a tiny, handmade caravan parked on Alan's parent's farm in Corrigin, it slowly dawned on them that they could now own a large, spacious home with views of the Bay. Mavis, who had pined for her dream home for years, had been collecting floor plans, and 'home beautiful' images of ideal nooks and crannies in homes most of her married life. She not only had a big scrapbook but she also had a big vision that had been incubating for decades.

*The Strand, Bunbury*

Alan and Mavis finally built their dream home, a glorious beach front, two-storey house, surprisingly equipped with four bedrooms and four bathrooms: big enough to house all the family at any time, especially during the Christmas season. But it took the humble pair fifteen years before they hung any more than mere curtain linings over their grand window panoramas.

The peaceful waters of Koombana Bay have brought these two enormous pleasure in their latter years; as have the frequent walks to the Bunbury Regional Entertainment Centre to enjoy the world quality shows, which can now come to Bunbury thanks to the generosity and fundraising of Alan and Mavis and his associates.

Not far away are the rabbits. They too occupy prime real estate and can be seen outside their beach-front residences at dusk enjoying the bay views

Mavis and Alan c.2006

## *Epilogue*

## *'There is nothing more important than family'*
*Alan Parsons*

## *Alan muses on his family*

On reflection, what are family values and how are they recorded? Family standards stem from many issues throughout life, and are built on love, compassion and ability to understand the people around you on a daily, yearly and forever basis.

We have four daughters; Julie, Eleanor and Susan were born when we were farming, and Gail, when we moved to Bunbury, each miraculously born on the 8th day of various months. If you think this involved some planning you would be wrong.

Mavis, who really knew nothing of farming, took on the task of parenting the children with the intention of doing it well, and it shows to this day. Her ability to teach and nurture the unique qualities of each daughter, from babyhood until they went out to make their own mark in this world, was outstanding and leaves a lasting legacy.

It was through Mavis that we came to Bunbury, in 1959, and the opportunity to become involved in the performing arts for both herself and the girls was evident. Mavis's abilities to perform in singing and acting was only outshone by her costume design and production. She was duly recognised in the 1990s by being awarded a Life Membership of the Southwest Opera Company.

We have four unique and much-loved grandchildren in Rad, Jamey, Yasen and Sophie. Their achievements and individuality bears thinking about. We love each one and marvel at who they are. We are also proud great grandparents to Anna Blossom who is busy forging her path and Hamish, Scarlett, Xena, Huxley and Luis who have just begun.

## The children

*Julie c.1980*

Julie Parsons was born at Corrigin in 1953. Julie pursued a career in Visual Arts, attaining an MA in Creative Arts and has been a practicing artist and sculptor for many years with her work being shown both nationally and internationally. She has worked as an art and design lecturer and managed big budgets in the making of her public art commissions. Other commissions include costume and set design for festivals, opera, dance and and theatre in Melbourne, Perth and Bunbury.

Julie has also trained and danced with Spanish dance and danse orientale companies, performing both as a soloist and group member. Julie and Mavis worked and performed together on many occasions. Julie married Andrew Young and they have two sons, Rad and Yasen, and three grandchildren, Anna Blossom, Xena and Luis.

Eleanor Parsons, was born at Corrigin in 1955. Eleanor inherited Mavis's musicianship and showed great skill in flute, piano and violin. This and her love of complex problem solving, goal orientation, and planning has seen her emerge from a payroll officer job to a career working in developing and consulting IT solutions; first in an engineering department, then the banking and medical sectors, and mining industry. A keen swimmer, Eleanor competes in both solo and team swims in the Rottnest Channel Swim. She is involved in the Masters Swimming championships, frequently winning medals in her age group and breaking records, allowing her to appear some four times in the world's top 10 ranking swimmers. On her 60th birthday she broke the Australian national record in 800m freestyle.

*Eleanor c.1980*

*Susan c.1980*

Susan Thompson (née Parsons) was born at Corrigin in 1957. Susan showed a leaning towards the performing arts early in her life. She shows the same fascination and passion for music, dance, singing and acting as Mavis and has worked all her life passing on her love of language and the Performing Arts teaching English, Drama and Music to thousands of students, young and old. She has directed over thirty school musicals for the same duration. Sadly, Susan did not inherit one iota of numbers sense from her father but can boast being a recipient of the Paul Harris Fellowship from Rotary (as was Alan) in recognition for her work with the youth of the Great Southern. Susan is married to Graham Thompson and they have two daughters, Jamey and Sophie, and three grandchildren, Hamish, Scarlett and Huxley.

Gail Parsons, was born in Bunbury in 1960. Gail seems to have inherited her love of crafts, buying and selling, managing people and cycling from both Alan and Mavis. Her career has leaned towards working with numbers and managing people, firstly in a bank and then as a highly skilled office manager. In her spare time, Gail dabbles in all sorts of crafts and is a very astute Gumtree marketer but her main passion is sport. Gail has enjoyed challenges in competition basketball, and has swum the Rottnest Channel many times with Masters swimming groups. Gail has recently taken up cycling and has now no less than four Hawaiian Ride for Youth charity rides to her credit. Gail's partner is David Corney.

*Gail c.1980*

# *The grandchildren*

*Rad 2017*

Rad was born in Perth in 1981. His passion began with graphic design before becoming focussed on film and television production. Rad has a Bachelor's degree in Screen with a specialisation in cultural studies from Murdoch University. He received the Vice Chancellor's Commendation for Academic Excellence in 2014 and has won multiple awards for his documentary filmmaking and photography. His work has been shown at festivals locally and internationally and also screened on SBS and ABC television. Rad is also an intrepid traveller.

Yasen was born in Bunbury in 1984. Yasen also has a great mix of the creative and astute business man in him, with him qualifying as an Electrician/Instrument Technician which saw him pave a career in the mining and heavy industry sector. He is a lecturer at TAFE and also applies himself to the fabrication and installation of public art, working on commissions in Bunbury and Perth, including the realisation of Julie's design for the construction of a 20 metre (industrial strength) royal costume depicting the gown Queen Elizabeth II wore for her photograph in the 1950s. Yasen's partner is Valentina Di Candia and they are raising Yasen's daughter Anna Blossom and their children Xena and Luis.

*Yasen c.2009*

*Jamey 2017*

Jamey was born in Perth in 1984. Whilst at school, Jamey exhibited great academic and creative talents in many areas, including Performing and Visual Arts. After receiving a BA in Communication Studies, Jamey set off interstate where she acquired medical receptionist and computer skills that she could utilise in her overseas travels. She then met Richard Claffey in Scotland. She attended university and received an MA in Screenwriting, which saw her career shifting to film and television at the BBC. Jamey is now an experienced freelancer who offers script and development services tailored to suit the needs of production. Jamey married Richard Claffey in Glasgow where their son, Hamish was born. The family now live in Perth Western Australia where Jamey continues her freelance work and is also lecturing at Curtin University.

Sophie was born in Perth in 1988. Sophie's passion and aptitude for music and visual arts showed itself very early on in her life. She was playing guitar, singing, and writing her own material from the age of nine. As a pre-teen, her family travelled across Australia to support her many ventures at the Tamworth Country Music Festival, where she won awards for her original songs. She is now an accomplished professional singer and songwriter who runs a very successful music business. Sophie has branched out to include her other passion, makeup, and has built up her own professional make-up business. She is also a qualified primary school teacher. Sophie's partner is Brendan Crees, they are raising their children Scarlett and Huxley.

*Sophie 2017*

# Post-script

In early 2022, Alan and Mavis decided to go for two weeks of respite at Southern Plus, a residential aged care facility in East Fremantle, where they were able to continue their life together in a double room.

However, before the first week was up, Alan found himself in Fiona Stanley Hospital for emergency surgery. A condition of his release was for round the clock care, so he and Mavis decided to stay on at Southern Plus. Alan regained his health while Mavis faced her own challenges with dementia and a broken hip. Covid came and went.

On the 8th of September 2022, in a surprise acknowledgement of his community service through Bunbury Rotary, Alan was honoured to receive a rare Honorary Lifetime Membership.

On the 10th of January 2023, their 72nd wedding anniversary, both Alan and Mavis visited Christ Church in Claremont where they were married and, with much nostalgia, Alan was able to look over their original marriage certificates.

Whilst living at the home, Alan, with his charming, positive approach to life and insistence that things can be done better, stayed in the ear of the director of the facility until he was asked if he would like to join the newly-formed Southern Cross Consumer Advisory Committee. This position gave him renewed purpose.

Sadly, however, Alan had only attended two meetings when he passed away suddenly and peacefully on the 30 August, 2023, just three weeks after his brother Brian (8th August 2023).

Alan's elegant funeral was on the 8th of September 2023 where Rotary formed a guard of honour outside St Boniface Cathedral in recognition of his valued contribution.

His obituary, which appeared in two newspapers, the West Australian and the South Western Times, cited him as a 'fundraising guru'.

Alan's lifetime belief that 'hard work brings good luck' had served him well.

*Appendices*

# Appendix I

Warracknabeal Herald             3 December 1915

## A GOLDEN WEDDING

### MR. AND MRS. GEO. PARSONS

**NOTABLE FAMILY GATHERING**

### CONGRATULATIONS AND GOOD WISHES.

There was a large gathering at McCombes Hall on Monday night, when Mr and Mrs George Parsons, two old and highly respected residents of Warracknabeal, celebrated their golden wedding.

At the Invitation of the members of the family, friends from all parts of the district attended, and the unique celebration was of the most pleasant character.

The catering was in the hands of Mrs Watson and a sumptuous repast was served, and was thoroughly enjoyed.

Rev T. Alday presided, and beside him sat Mr and Mr Parsons, who are still active and enjoying fairly good health. The members of the family are: Mr James Parsons, Minyip; Mr George Parsons, Narrogin, West Australia; Mr Walter Parsons, Boolite; Mr Alfred Parsons, Sheep Hills; Mr Edward Parsons, Bangerang; Mr Herbert Parsons, Bangerang; Mr Francis Parsons, Sheep Hills; Mr Arthur Parsons, Warracknabeal; Mrs K. Jenkins, Linga; Mrs A.V. Newell, Minyip; Mrs Sharpe, Areegra; Miss Martha Parsons, of Warracknabeal.

The whole of these were present to do honour to their parents, with the exception of the son in West Australia, who was unable to attend. There are 11 grandchildren, and 32 of the number were present. Mr Parsons was 77 years of age last September.

George and Louisa Parsons

He landed in Victoria in 1854, and for the greater part of his life followed agricultural pursuits. Mrs Parsons was 71 years of age in April last. For 40 years they have lived in the WIMMERA.

At first, they settled about 3½ miles from Minyip, where they remained for 19 years and then moved to Sheep Hills. In that district, they lived up until 5 years ago when they retired from the active work of the farm and settled in Warracknabeal.

Mr and Mrs Parsons experienced all the trials and difficulties associated with the opening up of this part of the State and have lived to enjoy the fruits of their industry, surrounded by members of the family, all of who are in comfortable circumstances and highly respected. These old pioneers have worthily performed their part as parents and as citizens of the State, and they have the best wishes of many friends for the fullest measure of happiness in the eventide of their lives.

It is notable that the members of the family have all settled on the land and are devoting their energies to primary industries, thus following in the footsteps of their parents.

At the celebration, after the singing of the National Anthem, a telegram was read from Mr George Parsons of West Australia, conveying congratulations to his parents.

There was also a communication from Messrs Mitchell Bros and White asking Mr and Mrs Parsons to accept the heartiest good wishes on the occasion of their golden wedding.

The marriage lines, which were read by the chairman, showed that George Parsons, Wattle Hill, Portland Victoria, a native of Somerset-shire England, at age 23 years was married to Louise Pitts of Wattle Hill, aged 18 years her birthplace being Kent Somerset-shire England.

In proposing Health and happiness to Mr and Mrs Parsons, the chairman said he counted it a privilege and an honour to submit the toast. Rarely did it fall to the lot of anyone to have the opportunity of proposing a toast of this kind twice within 3 months but that had been his privilege. On behalf of all present he desired to express their hearty congratulations to Mr and Mrs Parsons on having been spared in a measure of good health to celebrate their golden wedding.

Last year Mr Parsons had a severe attack of illness, which caused a great deal of anxiety, but in the good providence of God he had been spared to reach this important point, after 50 years of happy married life. He had pleasure in wishing them many more happy years and further that each year might be happier than any that had gone before. (APPLAUSE)

Mr J Vaughan, Sheep Hills, in supporting the toast, expressed thanks for the opportunity that had been given him of being present at the gathering. He joined with the Chairman in the hope that Mr and Mrs Parsons might enjoy health and happiness for some years to come, and the enjoyment afforded by the presence around of their children and grandchildren. (APPLAUSE)

Mr Hewitt said it gave him great pleasure to be present to tender his congratulations to Mr and Mrs Parsons, whom he had known for over 30 years. It was remarkable that Mr Parsons looked just as he did years ago. He was one of these men who did not seem to get any older. He had been a splendid father and had bought up a large family.

In his cultivation of the soil Mr Parsons was a good farmer, and in all his dealings he was an upright man and respected for his many good qualities. He had reached that period of life when he was able to review the past and see all the way he had come. Few men were privileged to celebrate their golden wedding and Mr Parsons should be a happy man. No doubt he was a happy man. He had started practically behind scratch and had battled through life successfully. His record of achievement was an example for others to follow. Mr and Mrs Parsons had his very best wishes and hoped they would be spared for many years yet. (APPLAUSE)

Cr C. Potter supported the remarks of the previous speakers. He said he had come a long way to the present but he would have gone as far again to do honour to Mr and Mrs Parsons. He had grown up amongst the members of the family and in the early days their place was a second home to him and Mr and Mrs Parsons were very close friends. Despite the weight of years, they still looked well and he had the pleasure in wishing them many more happy days. (APPLAUSE)

The toast was enthusiastically honoured and cheers were given for the aged guests.

A song was contributed by Miss Kruger of Lubeck and was appreciated by the company.

Mr J.J. Murchunt proposed the health of the family. He remarked that he had done a lot of business with Mr Parsons and they always trusted one another. If young people had to go through the same experience as Mr and Mrs Parsons he doubted whether they would do so well as the guests had done.

From a humble beginning, they had to fight their way through life and the success they had achieved was highly creditable to them. Regarding the family he had found them straightforward and honourable and they had reason to feel proud of their parents. He heartily joined in wishing Mr and Mrs Parsons as well as the family long life and happiness. (APPLAUSE)

Mr J. Twyford tendered his congratulations to the aged bride and bridegroom. He was sure it must be a proud moment for them to meet with members of their family on such an auspicious occasion. He was acquainted with the sons and daughters and the whole of them were a credit to their parents and greatly admired. (APPLAUSE)

Mr Byron referred in his association with the family and he appreciated their good qualities. (APPLAUSE)

Mr A. Parsons briefly returned thanks for the way in which the toast had been honoured and for the kind remarks made.

Mr S. Atkin, on behalf of the family presented Mr and Mrs Parsons with two comfortable saddlebag chairs. He congratulated the parents on the success they had achieved in life and on their attainment of an honourable old age, which was being spent under very happy conditions.

Between Mrs Atkin and Mrs Parsons there had been a life-long acquaintanceship and it had been of the most pleasant kind. The family presented the chairs as a token of love and affection and they trusted their parents might be spared many years yet to appreciate the comfort which the gift would afford. (APPLAUSE)

Mr Vaughan was called upon to respond. Mr Parsons being too much overcome with emotion to speak. Remarking that this was one of the greatest honours that had been conferred upon him.

Mr Vaughan went back 30 years ago and alluded to some of the hardships and difficulties with which the pioneers had to contend. There were few farmers who had to cart their wheat more than 10 or 12 miles at the present time, but in the early days of settlement the grain had to be taken to Stawell. The farmer started with his load on Monday morning and did not get back till Saturday night.

Water had also to be carted long distances. Mrs Parsons had stood loyally by her husband and helped him in every way through all the trials and disadvantages, which were the lot of the pioneer. The spirit, which dominated these early settlers was greatly to be admired and they had rendered great service to the country.

In the natural order of things many had passed away, but it was pleasing to know that their descendants were taking up the work which they commenced and were carrying it on successfully. The children were following in the footsteps of their parents.

Most people in the Wimmera were now living in comfortable homes and enjoyed great advantages as contrasted with the lot of their parents. For those blessings, they had reason to be thankful. Great praise was due to the Mothers who assisted in building up the homes in this country and who had taken so much interest in the welfare of their children.

Mr and Mrs Parsons had worked together with mutual love and sympathy for 50 years and it had proved to be a very happy union. On their behalf, he thanked the family for their thoughtful gift, which he was sure would be greatly appreciated. He felt confident that what was uppermost in the hearts of the parents was a feeling of thankfulness to God for his blessings that had been bestowed upon them and of the gratitude for the unbroken family that surrounded them. He trusted that the old couple might be spared to celebrate their jubilee. (LOUD APPLAUSE)

Mr Parsons senior... with some effort made a few remarks, though he was much affected. He said he was pleased to see so many of his old friends present to do him the honour. He was thankful that he had such good family and he was deeply moved by their kindness. It was a great pleasure for him to be spared so long and he thanked God for the blessings bestowed upon him and Mrs Parsons. (APPLAUSE)

Mr Hewitt proposed the health of the chairman and Mr Alday having responded, this part of the proceedings was closed with doxology.

The hall was then cleared and dancing was indulged in for some hours, good music being provided by Mr A. C. Taylor's orchestra. Mr and Mrs Parsons were recipients of many presents including a number of cheques.

# Appendix II

**Warracknabeal Herald** — March 1926

# Over the Roads by Motor Car

## A NOTABLE TRIP FROM WESTERN AUSTRALIA TO WARRACKNABEAL, VIC

### FROM THE DIARY ENTRIES BELONGING EDITH PARSONS

Mr and Mrs G.F. Parsons, with Mr and Mrs J.P. Myers, last week motored over 2,200 miles from Narrogin in West Australia to Warracknabeal, their only mishaps being one puncture and a broken spring. Mr Parsons is a brother of the well-known family of farmers in this district, where he was born, and a son of Mrs G. Parsons, of Devereux Street, Warracknabeal.

Mrs Parsons, Snr, who is now over 70 years of age, had not seen her son for several years and was naturally delighted at the reunion.

The following, very interesting, diary, was kept by Mrs Parsons on the trip over, and is as follows:

Saturday, March 6 - We left Narrogin at 5 pm and had a good run through to Bruce Rock, arriving there about 11.30 pm: 110 miles.

Sunday, March 7 - Left again in the morning at 8.30: very hot and sultry, with thunderstorms about. A heavy storm passed across Coolgardie and we ran into very heavy roads, before reaching Coolgardie, arriving there at 8 pm, Sunday evening. I do not believe there are six buildings in the main street of Coolgardie with the roof on; beautiful buildings at one time, and now nothing left but the bare walls. Every vestige of timber and iron has been taken away and sold. We travelled 224 miles today.

Monday, March 8 - We left here at 6.30 am. The proprietor of the hotel was good enough to get out of his bed at that early hour and pilot us out of the town and put us on the right road to Norseman, our next place of call. The roads were very heavy all the way through to Norseman, owing to the heavy storm that had passed over this part on the Sunday. We travelled on about 30 miles and then stopped and had breakfast. We boiled the billy, made toast, and had a good breakfast, and then on again. At lunchtime we stopped once more, had an hour's rest and off again.

The country is very changeable; beautiful soil that I believe would be impossible to beat if only the rainfall was high enough. It is hills and dales all the way, and since leaving Norseman we have run out of the wet roads. While the roads are wet the car slips and slides as though running on ice, and the man at the wheel has a trying time. We camped well and truly in the Australian bush on Monday night - pitched camp I suppose would be the boyish style of putting it. We travelled 178 miles on the Monday, but it was a good day's trip considering the early part of the day. This was our first night in the tent, and although very cold, we thoroughly enjoyed it.

The men folk pitched our tent with a rope from the side of the car and tied it to a convenient tree and with our Coolgardie stretchers, Mrs Myers and myself had only to close our eyes and imagine we were in the Metropole Hotel, Perth. The men folk made a bed of leaves two or three feet high by the side of the tent and covered themselves with rugs and declared they preferred it to the city hotels; their worst trouble being their inability to 'turn out the lights'. Old Sol always made a point of doing this himself about 5.30 am and, of course, this was the time they had themselves arranged to arise. They had, therefore" to sleep the night through with the full glare of the lights well turned on.

Another thing that annoyed them considerably was the negligence of 'Boots', who never once had their boots cleaned ready for them, although they were always most careful to place them well and truly outside!

Tuesday, March 9 - Had a drink of tea and a biscuit and left camp about 6 am. The country changes very rapidly, but it is all good, and some wonderful scenery. We travelled about 40 miles and then stopped for breakfast".

On we went again, this time over a salt lake on a road so beautifully smooth that the speedometer stood at 40 miles an hour the whole way across. The lake was dry and George reckoned it would make an ideal trotting track or football ground. At 11 am we came to Belladonna station. Here there are grapevines that were planted 40 years ago, and still bearing heavily; also there is a 'wooden python' - a piece of timber that in growing had twined around another piece, and the inner piece being removed left it a perfect-imitation of a 'python'. A new station home was in course of erection here. Of course it must be very lonely, but they appeared very happy and contented. We're just on the border of the Nullarbor Plains at this station, and from here on the road is almost perfect. Two hundred and fifteen (215) miles were travelled today.

Wednesday, March 10 - Left camp this morning about 5.30 am and travelled about 40 to 45 miles before breakfast - just by way of an appetiser for breakfast, so our men folk informed us. It was beautiful once we were going, and they always gave us a cup of tea before we started. The country we passed through today almost defies description. The track led us through thousands and thousands of acres of beautiful grass lands — still on the Nullarbor Plains! The grass is quite dry, of course, but is up to the sides of the car on either side and as thick as it can stand; the pity of it all is the shortage of water for stock purposes.

All through the route the Government have built iron sheds at intervals, and placed two, three or four iron tanks there. These were mostly full, and we had rainwater for tea the whole way through. The country is splendid, and the track through the Nullarbor Plains on the WA side perfect.

Mr Myers had four shots at dingoes coming across this morning, all in about an hour. He killed two, toppled one over, and made the other bark out for mercy. We travelled 215 miles again today, and crossed over the South Australian border 35 miles, camping once more on the Nullarbor Plains.

Thursday, March 11 - From here on the country rapidly grew drought-stricken and barren looking. We passed station after station, and there was not a vestige of grass to be seen. We travelled between six and seven hundred miles through this country, and did not notice one blade of grass. Here too, we crossed the 'Tardee Sands', one part of them is known as 'The Bullocky's Playground', and they are simply dreadful. There are 15 miles of these sands and anyone that has been through them will never forget them — they appear to be bottomless.

There are 14 miles of sand on the South Australian side of the Nullarbor Plains, and these also are very heavy. We reached Penong on Thursday night and stayed at the hotel longing for a hot bath but were informed the bathrooms had been locked up for two months as there was no water anywhere. Wherever you looked there were water tanks on wagons carting water.

All through SA they told us there had been no rain to do any good for 3½ years, and truly the country looked like it. We reached Port Augusta on Sunday evening, went round the Corong sands and waters — 187 miles of the most dreadful roads we had experienced all the way across (with the exception of nine miles across another salt lake where the speedometer again stood at 46 miles per hour).

From Kingston, we came on through Naracoorte, Goroke, and Horsham, and thence to Warracknabeal, having travelled 2,200 miles from when we left Narrogin. We rested one day only, and had a splendid trip from start to finish. The only mishap we had was the breaking of a main leaf in the front spring, which was repaired in about half an hour, and one puncture which only detained us a very few minutes.

We travelled in an Austin, and although it was severely tried more than once it never failed us. In one place in WA we came down a gorge between the cliffs, that to look at, you would say was impossible to take a car through, but it came down over the rocks and boulders without any trouble at all. This gorge is very steep, and I think dangerous, too, but we got safely down and breathed a sigh of relief to be on level ground again. We were really only travelling 10 days, for we rested one day. Many of our friends in WA prophesied when we were leaving that we would make the return journey by boat, but we had such a splendid trip across we are just as desirous returning by car as we were of coming over.

◆

*Appendix III*

The Corrigin Chronicle: (Vol. XVII No. 716)     Thursday 9th May 1940

# OBITUARY
## GEORGE FREDERICK PARSONS

The late G. F. Parsons.

The sudden death of Mr George Frederick Parsons at the Corrigin Hospital in the early hours of Saturday last, came as a distinct shock to his wife and family and numerous friends both here and at other centres where he was well known.

The deceased was born at Warracknabeal, Victoria, in 1871. His father, George Parsons, arrived in Australia about 90 years ago and at his passing, he left a family of nine sons and four daughters. In 1894 the late Mr Parsons married Edith Emily Bland and in 1908 arrived in Narrogin with his wife and young family, where they subsequently remained on a farming property situated a few miles out of town, until moving to the Corrigin district in 1930. He then acquired a property at Bendering afterwards moving into the township where he and his wife had conducted a business over the past three years. Meanwhile, the family of nine children had grown into manhood and womanhood and the majority are still in close association with the Corrigin district. They comprise five sons and four daughters viz., Les, Fred, Stan, Cliff, and Bert, Ivy, Ella (Mrs Ebsary), Eva (Mrs Hallet) and Maude. There are also thirteen grandchildren.

The funeral left the deceased's late residence at 4 pm on Sunday, and evidence of the wide respect and sympathy for the bereaved family was shown by the extraordinary large number of motor cars in the procession, many coming from Narrogin and other distant centres. The interment took place in the Methodist portion of the cemetery, the Reverend Worth officiating.

Pallbearers were J.R. Ashworth, J.P. Myers,

J. Gibson, H.A. Brown, J.J. James and Keith Ball, all of Narrogin. Funeral arrangements were conducted by Mr. A. Channon and many wreaths and other expressions of condolence were received, including those hereunder:

Loving Wife; Loving Family; Charlie, Maude, Les, Dorrie, Una, Jim, Clara; Trefort family and Arthur; Dawson Bradford; Fred, Lily, May, Alf; Mr and Mrs J. Keays and Ralph; J. Dougan and family; K.E. Ball; Billie and Dick and Corrigin Hospital staff; Mr and Mrs R. Bunker; Mr and Mrs F. Parry; Mr and Mrs A.W. Manning and family; Mr and Mrs Hawkins and family; Mr and Mrs Pond and family; Mr and Mrs Alf Channon and family; Laura, Vic, Alice and Mac; Roy and Allan (Denmark); Mr and Mrs Anderson; Mr and Mrs Myers; Mr and Mrs A. Spanney; Mr and Mrs Whyte and family; Mr and Mrs H.A. Brown and family; Cross Bros.; Mr and Mrs W. Parry; Mr and Mrs A.R. Matthews and family; Mr and Mrs H. Marsh and family, Mr and Mrs Jackson and family; Mr and Mrs Whitford and family; Mr and Mrs R.E. Rennie and family; Mr and Mrs Mickle and family; Alf, May and Eddie. And the boys of the Corrigin Hostel; President, Committee and members of the Narrogin Agricultural Society; management and staff of Elder, Smith and Co. Limited; Members of Corrigin Bowling Club; Chairman and Members and Staff of Corrigin Road Board; Chairman and Members of the Narrogin Road Board.

The late George Frederick Parsons was a man of parts and his influence in moulding the public and sporting activities of Narrogin (apart from his subsequent interest in those of Corrigin) was strongly in evidence during his long term of residence at that centre.

His capacity for work, kindly nature and readiness to shoulder the burden of public duty, naturally brought him into a prominence, which was maintained to the advantage of the community over many years.

It is not too much to say that in the heyday of his zealous efforts, every movement with which he was associated enjoyed full success and each was left with a record of honourable achievement when he retired to live in Corrigin.

In this regard the Narrogin Agricultural Society, Greater Sports Board and Trotting Club respectively, were particularly favoured through the strong influence of his sterling character, which was singularly free of concern for his own personal interests.

Big in stature, big in heart and seeing before him the straight path of duty, he was never known to shirk a responsibility or evade a principle. In every way he was genuine and naturally the various roles he filled in life were carried out with unflinching probity of purpose.

He was one of the best citizens, a capable farmer and grazier, whose knowledge was in keen demand at district shows, and a man to respect for his inherent strength of character and general attributes which found expression in the success of his public undertakings and happy personal contact with all sections of the public.

The district of Corrigin will be poorer for his death as that of Narrogin, was made poorer by the loss of his valuable services in 1930, when he left there amid heartfelt expressions of universal regret.

To the bereaved family the fullest sympathy is extended on all sides. The loss of his brave companionship and kindly direction in all affairs of domesticity is far greater than that sustained by his friends, yet withal it is more than an episode of passing sadness even with them. How much more will it be to his loving wife and family. Their one consolation is the knowledge that they do not mourn alone.

# Appendix IV

# Edith and George Parsons' family
## Alan remembers:

*4:15 The Parsons family late 1930s*
*Top right: Les, Fred, Cliff, Stan, Ella, George, Edith, Ivy, Bert, Eva, Maud*

### Ivy Parsons 1895-1965

Ivy appeared to have a normal brain. She knew family members as they came and went and knew the house routine, helping where she could, such as setting the table and bringing in the firewood. She rarely went to a doctor, but anything out of her comfort zone would make her very agitated. Edith gained great respect from everyone with her patience and care for Ivy all those years. No-one ever heard either of them complain. After Edith passed away in 1958, Ivy spent her last seven years in a nursing home. Apparently, some of the older family members were concerned that she would not accept the home but she was quite happy there. She had lost all her teeth years before but had her own way of communicating.

### Les Parsons 1896-1953
Married: Irene Bedwell 1916
Children: Audrey born 18th November 1917

Joined up for WWI (1914 -1918 war). Returned with ill health (his lungs were badly affected). Had several vocations managing Stock agencies and farms. He also managed a fuel company and went to Kalgoorlie prospecting for gold.

### Fred Parsons 1898-1974
Married: Mabel Ebsary 1918
Children: Gordon b.& d.1922, Lynn born 29th January 1926,
Neville born 10th April 1936

Farmed on his father's property in Narrogin. Fred bought a farm at Belka near Bruce Rock where he went bankrupt and lost both this farm and his parent's property called Highfield at Narrogin. Fred then farmed next to Emoh Ruo at Bendering. Passionate about his horses, he once travelled by taxi from Perth to an emergency with his horses on his farm and back again - an unheard of seven-hour round trip in a Perth taxi. He was a good horseman but drank and gambled too much. Shifted to Armadale but eventually went bankrupt again. Moved to Carnarvon and drove taxis. Due to a difficult situation Fred and Mabel, raised their granddaughter, Jane.

Two sons Lynn and Neville. Lynn drove a truck in Perth then joined the Air Force. Got allocated a war service farm in Jerramungup and became a very successful pioneer in the district but sadly he succumbed to the affects of alcohol and died in 1986. Neville, a transport driver, unfortunately died in a tragic accident aged 34, leaving behind his daughter Jane, wife Rona and their two sons Clay and Bevan.

*Authors note:* Twenty years later, in an eerie echo of events Clay, then in his early 30s, also had a truck accident in roughly in the same lonely spot. But Clay, miraculously uninjured, managed to walk up the road to where his father had lost his life and gave him thanks for saving his.

### Ella Parsons  1901-1974
Married: Wilf Ebsary 1934

Ella's vocation was nursing, all her working life. She became a Matron and worked in various hospitals including a stint in Marble Bar, the hottest place in WA, and that was before air conditioning. Wilf was not very well accepted in the family because of his relaxed attitude to work. He joined the Army, but it is unclear as to whether he left Australia. Wilf had various jobs in different towns, which is why Ella worked in different hospitals. He lost both his legs with illness and died in an old men's home in the late 1970s.

### Stan Parsons  1903-1979
Married: Olive Fairhead in 1925
Children: Beryl born 9th Nov 1925, Doug born 13th June 1929,
Colin born 15th July 1931, Phyllis born 18th Jan 1934

Stan moved to Corrigin in 1924 where he met Olive. They forever moved from farm to farm and from business to business. A news agency in Bayswater, a wood yard in Maylands, a bulldozer contractor business in Esperance, as well as trucks. He may not have been very successful in anything but he worked his boys, Colin and Doug hard in all his projects. The family lived in 19 homes, moving so many times that they had little or no social life.

### Cliff Parsons  1905-1984
Married: Alma Muir 5th February 1928. Divorced 1960s
Children: Alan born 12th February 1929, Brian born 7th June 1934
Married: Etta McDonald 19th August 1972 in Fremantle

Schooled in Narrogin then worked on the farms with his father and brothers. At about age 17 he joined Elders. The first few years it was the Depression and very hard going. Uncle Jack Shannon assisted where he could. Cliff seemed to have more confidence after settling at Kunjin and by the late 40s he had bought his own farm, making a mark in Corrigin by joining many of the social activities. Cliff was president of the Trotting Club, bowling club and as well as sitting on various committees. He chaired the Masonic factor for 12 months. When Cliff retired to Perth he was probably too young. He found it difficult to fit in and made several wrong decisions; when his marriage fell apart they divorced in the late 60s. He married Etta McDonald in 1972, then his health failed.

### Joseph Bert Parsons 1910-1947
Married: Jean Hawkins 1935
Children: Ray born 1st September 1939,
Kaye born 4th June 1942, Les born 10th December 1945

In Corrigin cemetery lay two babies in the same grave, James Parsons b/d. 1935 and Patricia Parsons b/d. 1937. Ray tells the story of his mothers concern for his health as a baby because he was born very thin. Times were difficult and nutrition through pregnancy was perhaps not understood. Bert spent time at Emoh Ruo, finally buying a farm west of Corrigin in early 1940 but by the late 1940s he had sold the Corrigin farm and had bought a farm in Three Springs, where he then lived.

### Eva Parsons 1913-2009
Married: Tom Hallett 1931. Divorced 1940s
Children: Carlton born 20 September 1931,
John born 12th May 1933, Robyn born 20th September 1937
Married: Jim Trott 1946

Tom was not accepted by the family because of a poor attitude to work. He joined the Army in 1940 and returned 1945. In the meantime, Eva had worked hard at various jobs. Eva divorced Tom and married Jim Trott in 1946. Jim and Eva worked hard, mainly trapping rabbits on the Nullarbor for weeks on end. Jim died in 1977. Eva passed away in a Mandurah nursing home aged 96, enjoying a cigarette and a glass of beer.

### Maude Parsons 1915-1952
Married: John Horbury 1944

Maude helped her mother on the farms and in the Hostel then went to live in Perth, working in various hotels and at different related jobs. John was considered a no-hoper by the family, only lasted a short time. Maude may have died a lonely alcoholic.

# Appendix V

Lynn Parsons 1945

Fred Parsons 1918

# *Lynn Parsons and the 1950s Soldier Settlement Scheme in Jerramungup WA*

George F. Parsons' grandson Lynn was the only of one of several Parsons boys to be called up to fight in World War II. The government required the others to contribute to the war effort as farmers. When Lynn Parsons, an air force mechanic, returned prospects were pretty grim until the 1950s, when the Commonwealth Government opened up land for settlement. According to the *ABC Rural* news on 25 April 2016, the resettlement project was the largest in the world at that time. Approximately 150 soldiers were granted land to farm, and although a number were unable to sustain this lifestyle, some did. Over a period of ten years, 141 farms were completed; however, only half-a-dozen families remained on the land.

Tyne Logan wrote the *ABC Rural* news article describing the commemoration of the scheme telling of the eight ex-servicemen who were sent to Jerramungup. Lynn Parsons was one such fortunate soldier, and his farming background laid the foundation for the farming community of Jerramungup.

Logan interviewed Lynn's son, Rex Parsons, who was brought to the farm by his mother as a six-week-old baby. In the article, Rex explained the difficulties farming presented to the 'Mad Eight' (as the soldiers were referred to at the time), but one difficulty stands out;

> *"When they came here the place was just moving with rabbits, so they had all that to contend with — not just developing the farms."*

Rex added to the report:

> *"I'm a farmer, it's in my blood, my parents are farmers, my brother's [Kim] still farming here on what was our original farm. Now I've got my son here farming with us, and luckily, we have a two-year-old grandson here with us as well so the future is pretty much assured."*

Rex and his wife Tracey now live in the homestead once occupied by Major Colin Cameron

# Appendix VI

A flurry of activity began in early 2016 when Alan decided a big party was in order as both Mavis and Queen Elizabeth II were turning 90 within a month of each other. Mavis, like many of the women in her family, had aligned herself with the Monarch, (this would not be the first birthday she celebrated wearing a crown).

Alan handed the idea over to his family who each did what they could in their own unique ways to bring the event into realisation.

The invitation requested the following;

**DRESS CODE: Ostentatious**

AMBASSADORS, MINISTERS & GOVERNORS: Wear full official attire
MILITARY: Uniforms & decorations expected
GENTLEMEN: Afternoon hats and gloves
LADIES: Expensive jewellery, hats & gloves please

**GIFTS OF SAPPHIRES SET IN GOLD WILL ONLY BE ACCEPTED**

Everyone arrived suitably dressed for the occasion aided and abetted by Mavis's extraordinary period millinery collection.

Susan entertained the crowd with a letter she composed as written by the Queen to Mavis comparing their life journeys in the most absurdly bizarre and nonsensical ways. Sentences like: "We have both arrived at this point in our lives relatively unscathed and still with our dignity and continence in tact! One cannot cannot ask for much more than that!"

The laughter flourished for sometime into the evening.

Mavis' 90th birthday invitation, 2016 Invitation
Artwork: Rad Young

Appendix 305

# Bibliography

## Books and articles

*A golden wedding anniversary.* Retrieved from http://nla.gov.au

Anderson, Laurie 1999, *Windows on the wheatbelt*, Access Press, Bassendean

Astbury, Heidi & Chadwick, Lyn 1987, extracted from *Noman's Lake – A collection of memories.* Retrieved from www.narrogin.wa.gov.au

Automotive Holdings Ltd, 1987, from *Linking the strength of Western Australia's largest automotive group*

Bolton, G.C. 1986, *Mitchell, Sir James (1866-1951)* article in Australian dictionary of biography, vol. 10, (MUP) National Centre of Biography, Australian National University, published first as a hardcopy. Retrieved from www.adb.anu.edu.au

*Boots Chemist.* Retrieved from www.boots-uk.com

*Bramall Hall.* Retrieved from www.stockport.gov.uk

*Caroline Agnes* passenger list for Bland family. Retrieved from www.oocities.org

*Charles Hull.* Retrieved from www.charleshull.com.au

Chuk, Florence 1987, *The Somerset years: government-assisted emigrants from Somerset and Bristol who arrived in Port Phillip/Victoria, 1839-1854*, Pennard Hill publications, Ballarat

*Claude de Bernales.* Retrieved from www.adb.anu.edu.au

*Collie.* Retrieved from www.collierivervalley.com.au

*Corrigin.* Retrieved from www.corrigin.wa.gov.au

Cranny, Bill 1989, *Selling trucks in WA*, Aug issue of 'Western Transport', pp.43 - 45

Criddle, Roy 2016, *Lucky kid: a memoir of Corrigin and Narrogin*, self-published, WA

Facey, A.B. 1981, *A fortunate life*, Fremantle Press, revised edn, Penguin 2005, Fremantle

Farm machinery dealers association, 31 June 1977 *Farmers Weekly.* Retrieved from www.farmweekly.com.au

Ferguson, Beth December 2014, The Alan Parsons life project, *Business Focus*, Bunbury Chamber of Commerce

Garden, Don 2010, *The Federation drought of 1895-1903.* Retrieved from www.climatehistory.com.au

Gregg, Alison 1993, *The hope of the future: The kindergarten union and the campaign for children's libraries in Western Australia.* Retrieved from www.iier.org.au

Gregg, Alison 1993, *Issues In educational research 3 (1),* pp.17-33. Retrieved from www.iier.org.au

Haebich, Anna 1988, *For their own good: Aborigines and Government of Western Australia 1900-1940*, p.27, UWA Publishing, Perth

Haig, Ross 1982, *Corrigin: Pioneering days and beyond*, Shire of Corrigin, Corrigin.

Heritage Council of Western Australia 2009, *Assessment Documentation Dryandra Woodland Settlement*. Retrieved from www.inherit.stateheritage.wa.gov.au

Hofmaier, Keith 1976, *Mallee memories*, published by Warracknabeal Herald, Victoria

Hough, David & Finlay, Len (eds) 2007, Obituaries: Remarkable story of debt repayment. *The West Australian*, Perth

Ling, Julie et al. 2013, *Corrigin: Moments in time 1913-2013: a visual journal of life in Corrigin over 100 years*. Corrigin Centenary Committee, Corrigin.

Logan, Tyne 2016, *WA soldier settlement stays in the family*. Retrieved from www.abc.net.au

McPharlin, Walter Raymond 1972, *Honorary royal commission appointed to inquire into hire purchase and other agreements*, State Law Publisher, Perth.

*Minyip*. Retrieved from www.minyip.com.au.

Mollemans & Beeston 1992, *Distribution and ecological significance of on-farm bushland remnants in southern wheatbelt region of Western Australia*, Dept. of Agriculture, Perth.

*Muir family tree*. Retrieved from www.oneil.com.au

Munday, Bruce 2017, *Those wild rabbits: How they shaped Australia*. Mile End, Wakefield Press, South Australia

*Narrogin Road Board Honour Board*. Retrieved from www.narrogin.wa.gov.au

*Nesta shipwreck*. Retrieved from www.environment.gov.au

*Pitts family*. Retrieved from www.westerndistrictfamilies.com

*Rabbit-proof fence*. Retrieved from www.wanowandthen.com

Rockman, Colin 2005, *Wheels of fortune: The life and times of the Automotive Holdings Group*, pp.128, 211. Automotive Holdings, West Perth

*Sandford pioneers*. Retrieved from www.swvic.org

Schofield, Julienne 2012, *The fallen leaves of the Parsons family*. Self-published, Benalla

State Heritage Council, *Double State heritage listing for Corrigin*. Retrieved from www.stateheritage.wa.gov.au/news/2012/06/29/double-state-heritage-listing-for-corrigin

*The West Australian* 5 May 1940 death notices. Retrieved from www.myheritage.com

Treloar, John & Shaw, Peter 2006, *The kilted battalion: the history of 16th infantry battalion (the Cameron Highlanders of Western Australia)*. 16th Battalion the Cameron Highlanders of Western Australia Association, Kardinya

*WA drought broken*. Retrieved from www.trove.nla.gov.au

*WA Government Gazette* (1925). Retrieved from www.nla.gov.au

*Yarriambiack heritage*. Retrieved from www.yarriambiack.vic.gov.au

## *Interviews, correspondence and diary entries*

Drage, Graham 2001, *Underground mutton* (a family history, author's possession)

Elliot, Anne 2016-17, Written research supplied

Golding, Graham & Jenny 2017, email correspondence

Jones, Wally 2017, email correspondence

Matthews, Yvonne & Bill 2016-17, correspondence and interviews

McGinnity, June 2016-17, oral history

Muir, Daryl 2017, interview

Muir, Kelly 2017, material collection

Parsons, Alan 2009-17, oral and written history

Parsons, Julie 1976-96, diary entries

Parsons, Mavis 1980-17, oral history

Schofield, Julienne 2017, personal collections of researched and written material

Thompson, Susan 2017, written research supplied

## *Newspaper clippings in family's possession*

*Elders Weekly 70th Anniversary Edition*, Machinery advances beyond imagination: History of Machinery, 27 August 1992, pp. 44 & 46

*South Western Advertiser* 8 December 1949

*The Corrigin Chronicle* 9 May 1940, Obituary G.F. Parsons, vol. xvii (716), p. 2

*The West Australian* 28 December 1993, *$26m paid back with interest* (headline)

*Warracknabeal Herald* 3 December 1915, *A golden wedding Mr. and Mrs. George Parsons*

*Warracknabeal Herald* March 1926, *From Western Australia to Warracknabeal, Vic - Over the Roads by Motor Car*

## *Archives*

Brunswick Agriculture Show archives

# *Photographs, Illustrations and artworks*

All photographs are from family collections except where credited otherwise.

Painted images of rabbits throughout: Julie Parsons.

**ill i.** Page 22 - Thomas Austin. Graphite rendered drawing after the portrait in Victoria and its Metropolis, past and present. 190x220mm; artist Julie Parsons, 2017

**ill ii.** Page 24 - The Duke of Edinburgh rabbit shooting at Barwon Park, Victoria. Graphite rendered drawing after 1867 engraving by N Chevalier. 250x190mm; artist Julie Parsons, 2017

**ill iii.** Page 31 - The old wagon on the Minyip property with the faint memory of Martha doing a jig to entertain her siblings. A family photograph of the old wagon on the original property inspired the drawing, 200x290mm; artist Julie Parsons, 2017

**ill iv.** Page 43 - Gouache painting of rabbits; artist Julie Parsons 2017

**ill v.** Page 124 - Imaginary drawing of sisters Annie and Ethel at the Kondinin Co-op store in the 1920s, inspired by historic photograph near the pioneer wall in Kondinin. 200x290mm; artist Julie Parsons, 2017

**ill vi.** Page 172 - Boots Chemist, Windsor. Graphite rendered drawing (detail) referencing 1900s postcard image; 175x140mm; artist Julie Parsons, 2017

**ill vii.** Page 250 - *Alma the hat box drawers*. A homage to Grandmother Alma Parsons, design and finish by Julie Parsons, construction by Alan Parsons with Julie Parsons. Fabric covered drawers in a pink lime washed timber frame. There are secret jewellery compartments behind eyes, lips, and neck. 180x60x60cm, 1995

**ill viii.** Page 278-9 - Jetty Baths Bunbury in 1940. Graphite rendered drawing (detail) referencing a photograph in the City of Bunbury Port history collection. 230x165mm; artist Julie Parsons, 2017

**ill ix.** Page 278-9 - Mosaics set limestone seawalls around Marlston Hill. The mosaics are part of a public art commission titled *One Century of Swimming Lessons*, made from handmade and handpainted tesserae, set in brass frames and inlaid into limestone walls. Four mosaics 100x20cm: two mosaics 20x55cm; artist Julie Parsons 2001.

www.ingramcontent.com/pod-product-compliance
Lightning Source LLC
Chambersburg PA
CBHW051333110526
44591CB00026B/2983